DEC   2012

A NEW WORLD POWER

America from 1920 to 1945

DOCUMENTING AMERICA
THE PRIMARY SOURCE DOCUMENTS OF A NATION

A NEW WORLD POWER
America from 1920 to 1945

EDITED BY JEFF WALLENFELDT, MANAGER, GEOGRAPHY AND HISTORY

Published in 2013 by Britannica Educational Publishing
(a trademark of Encyclopædia Britannica, Inc.)
in association with Rosen Educational Services, LLC
29 East 21st Street, New York, NY 10010.

Distributed exclusively by Rosen Educational Services.
For a listing of additional Britannica Educational Publishing titles, call toll free (800) 237-9932.

First Edition

Britannica Educational Publishing
Marilyn L. Barton: Senior Coordinator, Production Control
Steven Bosco: Director, Editorial Technologies
Lisa S. Braucher: Senior Producer and Data Editor
Yvette Charboneau: Senior Copy Editor
Kathy Nakamura: Manager, Media Acquisition
Jeff Wallenfeldt: Manager, Geography and History

Rosen Educational Services
Hope Lourie Killcoyne: Executive Editor
Nelson Sá: Art Director
Cindy Reiman: Photography Manager
Karen Huang: Photo Researcher
Brian Garvey: Designer, Cover Design
Introduction by Jeff Wallenfeldt

Library of Congress Cataloging-in-Publication Data

A new world power: America from 1920 to 1945/edited by Jeff Wallenfeldt.—1st ed.
  p. cm.—(Documenting America: the primary source documents of a nation)
Includes bibliographical references and index.
ISBN 978-1-61530-694-7 (library binding)
1. United States—History—1919–1933—Sources—Juvenile literature. 2. United States—History—1933–1945—Sources—Juvenile literature. 3. United States—Politics and government—1919–1933—Sources—Juvenile literature. 4. United States—Politics and government—1933–1945—Sources—Juvenile literature. 5. United States—Foreign relations—20th century—Sources—Juvenile literature. 6. World War, 1939–1945—United States—Sources—Juvenile literature. I. Wallenfeldt, Jeffrey H.
E785.N48 2013
973.91—dc23

2012003795

Manufactured in the United States of America

On the cover (main): Mexican artist Diego Rivera, known for his bold, politically themed large-scale murals, created this fresco depicting work at an automotive plant—America's burgeoning industry of mass production—as part of his Detroit Industry Fresco Cycle, 1932, for the Detroit Institute of Arts. *Apic/Hulton Archive/Getty Images*

On the cover (document): The Social Security Act was legislation enacted by the U.S. Congress in 1935 to provide old-age benefits to be financed by a payroll tax on employers and employees. *Record Group 11, General Records of the U.S. Government, 1778–2006, National Archives and Records Administration*

On page viii: Franklin Delano Roosevelt, the only U.S. president elected to office four times, led the country through two of the greatest crises of the 20th century: the Great Depression and World War II. He is seen here in the 1930s, delivering one of his regular national radio broadcasts, which would come to be known as Fireside Chats. *Stock Montage/Archive Photos/Getty Images*

On pages 1, 15, 22, 30, 40, 49, 56: The Works Progress Administration (WPA) employed many artists as part of its mission to provide meaningful jobs for the unemployed. This painting, *c.* 1938, by artist Moses Soyer, depicts WPA artists at work. During its eight-year existence the WPA put some 8.5 million people to work (over 11 million were unemployed in 1934) at a cost to the federal government of approximately $11 billion. *MPI/Archive Photos/Getty Images*

CONTENTS

3

7

26

36

37

INTRODUCTION

For much of the 19th century, news—good and bad—traveled quickest via telegraph. By the beginning of the 20th century, an expanding telephone network provided word-of-mouth delivery for some, but readers, as they had long done, still turned to newspapers to keep up with events. In the 1920s, radio—the first electronic mass medium—joined the national conversation, with several networks linking listeners across the country before the end of the decade. Herbert Hoover, who had been in charge of radio policy from 1922 to 1925 as the secretary of commerce, was the president in 1929 when the news went out that the stock market crashed. By 1932, drastic declines in industrial production, continuing recession, and the barest of bear markets, among other factors, culminated in the biggest economic downturn in the history of the United States, the Great Depression. By 1933 one in four Americans was jobless. Times were desperate.

Hoover was a competent administrator but not the skillful politician that the country needed to lead it out of the depression. His replacement as president, the charismatic Franklin D. Roosevelt, was, and Roosevelt used radio to calm the fears of Americans in a series of intimate addresses from the White House that became known as the Fireside Chats, the first one of which aired March 12, 1933. In soothing tones and simple, direct language, Roosevelt explained the country's predicament and how he planned to use the New Deal to get Americans back on their feet.

Many decades later we cannot crowd around a radio in the living room with loved ones to hear Roosevelt's words for the first time, but we can experience them first-hand in print. In this volume, Roosevelt still speaks to us through transcripts of two Chats. One summarizes the legislation enacted and actions taken during the remarkable first "Hundred Days" of his administration; another, from the summer of 1934, looks at the relief, recovery, and reform that seemed to promise a more hopeful future. In presenting the history of the United States from 1920 to 1945 through primary source documents—the words of its leaders and people—this book turns repeatedly to Roosevelt, which should come as little surprise. Serving an unmatched four terms in the Oval Office, Roosevelt guided America through not only the Great Depression but also World War II. So, in addition to Fireside Chats, this volume offers Roosevelt's address to Congress in 1935 in which he proposed the creation of Social Security; the 1936 address in which he outlined his "Good Neighbor Policy" toward Latin America; his famous "Four Freedoms" speech from 1941, on the eve of American involvement in World War II; and the executive order from the same year with which he sought to eliminate discrimination in war-related industry.

Likewise, Roosevelt's signature is on the Atlantic Charter, the proposal for a better world he and British Prime Minister Winston Churchill formulated in a meeting at sea in 1941. That meeting cemented the wartime Anglo-American partnership that would first take the form of armaments provided by the "neutral" United States to Britain and later see them as Allies in the fight against Nazi Germany, Fascist Italy, and totalitarian Japan. Among others, the United States and Britain were joined in that fight by the Soviet Union, and in 1945, Roosevelt, Churchill, and Soviet leader Joseph Stalin ("the Big Three") met in the Crimea to set forth their plans for the settlement of the conflict and the postwar world. The result of that gathering, the Yalta Agreement, is another of the primary sources offered here to immerse the reader in the drama of the precarious fast-changing times.

Pivotal to understanding the period though it was, Roosevelt's voice was, however, just one among many that shaped a United States in the process of fashioning itself into the world's preeminent military and economic power. The reflections of Roosevelt's thought and influence included here, then, are just some of the primary sources interwoven with a historical narrative that presents a description and analysis of the period, its events, and its most important issues. That narrative provides a framework for approaching the documents that allows the reader to come to his or her own conclusions regarding their meaning. When the documents are short, they are presented whole, within the narrative. More often, excerpts are provided that give a flavour of the document, which is then presented more fully in the Appendix. Specific introductions for each document provide additional context.

The story begins at the end of World War I, when many Americans seemed anxious to distance themselves from world events and were especially threatened by the potential spread of the communist ideology that underpinned the newly emergent Soviet Union. The result was the Red Scare of 1919–20, which led to widespread condemnation and arrest of "agitators." The flimsiness of some of the accusations of traitorous activity was satirized by humourist Robert Benchley in a *Nation* magazine article, "The Making of a Red." Fundamentalism, a conservative belief in a literal, unchanging interpretation of the Bible, became a huge force in American Protestantism and society at this time, playing a significant role in the adoption in 1919 of the Eighteenth Amendment, which prohibited the manufacture, sale, or transportation of intoxicating liquors. Ultimately, Prohibition would be impossible to enforce as speakeasies (secret drinking establishments) flourished, often supplied by gangsters, such as Chicago's Al Capone, who fought violent turf wars. Fundamentalist disapproval of the teaching of the Darwinian theory of evolution also was at the centre of the era's famous Scopes "Monkey" trial. The tension between the fundamentalist and modernist approaches to religion and the world was the subject of an influential sermon by the Rev. Harry Emerson Fosdick, a liberal Protestant minister with an interdenominational congregation in New York City, who concluded, "There is one thing I am sure of: courtesy and kindness and tolerance and humility and fairness are right. Opinions may be mistaken: love never is."

By the 1920s Americans were well used to the boom and bust cycles of capitalism. When agriculture, business, and industry flourished in the United States, the sound of success was thunderous, echoing across the globe. But the American economy also periodically slid into disastrously deep troughs, as it did in the financial panics and depressions of 1819, 1837, 1857, 1873, and 1893. Just after World War I, however, the U.S. economy was as red hot as the all-American music that provided one of the names used to characterize the period—the Jazz Age. The era's better known moniker, the Roaring Twenties, was even more descriptive of the country's boisterous business and social climate. Profits were up, wages were climbing, too, and the stock market was stratospheric, with an unprecedented number of prosperous Americans along for the giddy ride. Republican Warren G. Harding, who had entered the White House in 1920 promising a "Return to Normalcy," presided over much of these flush times, though he seems not to have kept too careful an eye on some in his administration. It was on his watch that the Tea Pot Dome scandal unfolded, chronicled in *Forum* magazine by Sen. Thomas J. Walsh, who helped expose what was the nation's biggest ever influence-peddling scam, one in which Secretary of the Interior Albert Fall, "sold" oil rights to government land for personal gain. Calvin Coolidge, who

had succeeded to the presidency upon Harding's untimely death, famously said that "the chief business of the American people is business," but in a 1923 Memorial Day speech, when he was still vice president, he qualified his support of largely unfettered capitalism by saying, "no private enterprise can succeed unless the public welfare be held supreme." Earlier in the same speech he said, "The most pressing requirement of the present day is that we should...be content with a fair share, whether it be the returns from invested capital or the rewards of toil." But in the 1920s, with the economy humming and the stock-market singing, it seemed hard for Americans not to want more.

Farmers, especially those in the Great Plains, learned their lesson sooner than those in the cities. Huge wartime demand for American wheat had prompted many farmers to put more acreage under cultivation in the 1920s, borrowing to expand their holdings or converting stock-grazing land to crops. Overproduction resulted in declining prices. When prolonged drought in the early 1930s desiccated topsoil that was fragile in much of the region, the livelihoods, deeds, and dreams of many farmers disappeared. The desperation and strength of those displaced by the resulting Dust Bowl was the subject of John Steinbeck's era-defining novel *The Grapes of Wrath*; the plight of southern tenant farmers was given a more clinical but no less revealing description in the federal government's Report on Conditions in the South. And at the end of the 1920s the pain spread well beyond the farm as buying stock on margin (more excessive speculative borrowing) proved the undoing of countless Americans when the Wall Street market crashed amid a rapid succession of "black" sell-off weekdays, followed all too quickly by the onset of the depression.

The Roosevelt administration attacked the depression with an ongoing assault of experimental legislation, including the Agricultural Adjustment Act, described and explained by Henry Wallace, Roosevelt's secretary of agriculture and later vice president, in his Declaration of Interdependence radio address in June 1933. The act sought to raise the prices of crops by limiting production, but it required cooperation across the agricultural sector to succeed. As Wallace said, "Without that, no price-lifting effort can possibly work; because if there is no control of acreage, the better price increases the next year's planting and the greater harvest wrecks the price." New Deal legislation included the creation of the Federal Emergency Relief Administration to provide help for those struggling to survive, the Public Works Administration and the Civilian Conservation Corps to put millions back to work, and the National Recovery Administration to coordinate prices and wages. Conservatives criticized these efforts for introducing too much government intervention and institutionalizing socialism. Others, such as populist leaders Huey P. Long and Father Charles E. Coughlin, lambasted Roosevelt for not

doing enough. Long's Share-the-Wealth plan of economic distribution promised to make "every man a king" by limiting "the amount any one man can earn in one year or inherit to $1 million per person."

Partly in response to such criticism, the legislation often referred to as the Second New Deal was even more aggressive, most notably the creation of the Works Progress Administration. Among the principal beneficiaries of the New Deal was the labour movement, which received new protections in the National Labor Relations Act (Wagner Act) and the Fair Labor Standards Act. The labour movement also gained tremendous momentum when John L. Lewis and others broke from the American Federation of Labor in 1938 to form the Congress of Industrial Organizations, which became one of the major players in New Deal coalition. In his address as the chairman of the Congress's first convention, Lewis asked why anyone would oppose an organization such as the CIO, which "stands for orderly procedure and for a rational working out of the problems of modern industrial relationships... that is dedicated to the proposition of maintaining and supporting our democratic form of government... dedicated to the proposition of the right of investors to have a profit on their investment...asking only in return that the safeguards of the Constitution and the Bill of Rights be extended to cover the most lowly, humble worker, as a right, as a privilege for an American?"

Even as World War II raged in Europe, North Africa, and Asia, many Americans remained determined isolationists. As Roosevelt gradually increased American support of the Allies, his Republican opponent in the 1940 presidential race, Wendell Wilkie, accused him of maneuvering an unwilling nation too quickly toward war. "There have been occasions when many of us have wondered if he is deliberately inciting us to war," Wilkie said in his acceptance of the Republican nomination. "But while he has thus been quick to tell other nations what they ought to do, Mr. Roosevelt has been slow to take the American people into his confidence." Once the United States did become involved in the war, the internment of Japanese Americans in camps on the West Coast because of the security threat they allegedly posed raised a controversy that was ultimately addressed by the Supreme Court, which found the internment legally defensible. In one of the court's dissenting opinions, however, Judge Frank Murphy wrote that there was no "reliable evidence...to show that such individuals were generally disloyal, or had generally so conducted themselves in this area as to constitute a special menace to defense installations or war industries, or had otherwise by their behavior furnished reasonable ground for their exclusion as a group... Racial discrimination in any form and in any degree has no justifiable part whatever in our democratic way of life."

Roosevelt led the nation through the war and out of the Great Depression—as much by inspiring hope as through the specific legislation he brought about—but he did not live to see the true end of either. Moreover, his sudden death at the beginning of his fourth term left Harry S. Truman, the new relatively inexperienced vice president who ascended to the presidency, with the tremendous responsibility of deciding whether to use the new, secretly developed, monumentally destructive atomic bomb to end the war with Japan. When Truman announced the dropping of the bomb on Hiroshima, Japan, he not only foretold the end of the conflict, but he ushered in a new world in which the United States would hold a place of unprecedented prominence.

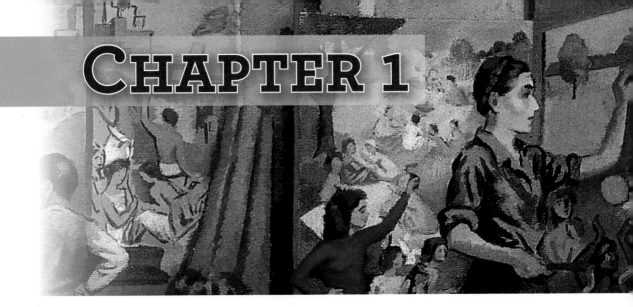

Chapter 1

The Postwar Republican Administrations

By August 1914—when Pres. Woodrow Wilson implored the American people to be "neutral in thought as well as deed" with respect to the outbreak in Europe of what would become World War I—the United States was already the greatest industrial power in the world. Yet its tradition of isolationism and its tiny standing army gave the Europeans excuse to ignore America's potential might. Ultimately, the United States would not only become involved in the war, but its contribution would have much to do with the Allied victory. The bells, flags, crowds, and tears of Armistice Day 1918 testified to the relief of exhausted Europeans that the killing had stopped and underscored their hopes that a just and lasting peace might repair the damage, right the wrongs, and revive prosperity in a broken world. Wilson's call for a new and democratic diplomacy, backed by the suddenly commanding prestige and power of the United States, suggested that the dream of a new day in world politics was not merely Armistice euphoria. But when Wilson was unable to convince Congress to allow the United States to join the newly created League of Nations, the country stepped off the world's political main stage.

POSTWAR CONSERVATISM

After World War I many Americans were left with a feeling of distrust toward foreigners and radicals, whom they held responsible for the war. The Russian Revolution of 1917 and the founding of the communists' Third International—a communist organization begun in Moscow in 1919 by Vladimir Lenin— further fanned American fears of radicalism. Race riots and labour unrest added to the tension. Thus, when a series of strikes and indiscriminate bombings began in 1919, the unrelated incidents were all assumed—incorrectly in most cases—to be communist-inspired. During the ensuing Red Scare, civil liberties were sometimes grossly violated and many innocent aliens were deported.

Document: Robert Benchley: "The Making of a Red" (1919)

The Red Scare of 1919-20 was the result partly of wartime passions as yet unabated and partly of an intensive propaganda campaign aimed at the Western countries by Russia after the October Revolution. The U.S. Justice Department gave the violent but short-lived movement official support, and "Palmer raids"–named after Attorney General A. Mitchell Palmer—occurred from time to time starting in the fall of 1919. These raids, involving countrywide mass arrests of political and labour agitators, came to a head on Jan. 2, 1920, when more than 2,700 people were taken into custody in 33 cities. The raids were terminated in May, but not until many aliens had been deported to Russia. Humorist Robert Benchley published some sardonic observations on the "Red Menace" in the Nation *early in 1919. The essay is reprinted here.*

You couldn't have asked for anyone more regular than Peters. He was an eminently safe citizen. Although not rich himself, he never chafed under the realization that there were others who possessed great wealth. In fact, the thought gave him rather a comfortable feeling. Furthermore, he was one of the charter members of the war. Long before President Wilson saw the light, Peters was advocating the abolition of German from the public-school curriculum. There was, therefore, absolutely nothing in his record which would in the slightest degree alter the true blue of a patriotic litmus. And he considered himself a liberal when he admitted that there might be something in this man Gompers, after all. That is how safe he was.

But one night he made a slip. It was ever so tiny a slip, but in comparison with it De Maupassant's famous piece of string was barren of consequences. Shortly before the United States entered the war, Peters made a speech at a meeting of the Civic League in his home town. His subject was: "Inter-urban Highways: Their Development in the Past and Their Possibilities for the Future." So far, 100 percent American. But, in the course of his talk, he happened to mention the fact that war, as an institution, has almost always had an injurious effect on public improvements of all kinds. In fact (and note this well — the government's sleuth in the audience did) he said that, all other things being equal, if he were given his choice of war or peace in the abstract, he would choose peace as a condition under which to live. Then he went on to discuss the comparative values of macadam and wood blocks for paving....

The Red Scare was over within a year, but a general distrust of foreigners, liberal reform movements, and organized labour remained throughout the 1920s. In fact, many viewed Republican Warren G. Harding's landslide victory in the 1920 presidential election as a repudiation of Pres. Woodrow Wilson's internationalism and of the reforms of the Progressive era.

Warren G. Harding, the president-elect, riding in a carriage with outgoing president Woodrow Wilson on the way to Harding's inauguration as the 29th president of the United States. Topical Press Agency/Hulton Archive/Getty Images

PEACE AND PROSPERITY

Harding took office with a clear mandate to restore business as usual, a condition he termed "normalcy." Americans wished to put reminders of the Great War behind them, as well as the brutal strikes, the Red Scare, and the sharp recession of Wilson's last years in office. Peace and prosperity were what people desired, and these would be achieved under Harding.

As part of his policy of returning America to prewar conditions, Harding pardoned many individuals who had been convicted of antiwar activities or for being radicals. His main concern, however, was business. Reversing progressive and wartime trends, the Harding administration strove to establish pro-business policies. Attorney General Harry M. Daugherty obtained injunctions against striking workers. The Supreme Court sided with management in disputes over unions, minimum wage laws, child labour, and other issues. Secretary of Commerce Herbert Hoover expanded the size of his department fourfold during the next eight years in attempts to foster business growth and efficiency and to encourage trade associations and business–labour cooperation. Secretary of the Treasury Andrew W. Mellon, one of the country's richest men, drastically cut taxes, especially on the wealthy (individual income taxes having begun just a few years earlier, in 1913, by virtue of the Sixteenth Amendment to the Constitution). Mellon also cut federal spending to reduce the national debt.

In foreign affairs the Harding administration tried to ensure peace by urging disarmament, and at the Washington Naval Conference in 1921 Secretary of State Charles Evans Hughes negotiated the first effective arms-reduction agreement in history. On the whole, however, the policies of the United States were narrow and nationalistic. It did not cooperate with the League of Nations. It insisted that Europeans pay their American debts, but in 1922 passed the Fordney–McCumber Tariff, which raised duties so high that foreigners had great difficulty earning

the necessary dollars. When immigration reached prewar levels (some 800,000 people entered the country between June 1920 and June 1921), Congress gave in to the protests of organized labour, which believed immigrants were taking jobs away from American citizens, as well as to the objections of business leaders and patriotic organizations, who feared that some of the immigrants might be radicals. Reversing traditional American policy, Congress passed first an emergency restriction bill and then in 1924 the National Origins Act. The act set a quota limiting the number of immigrants to 164,000 annually (150,000 after July 1, 1927); it discriminated against immigrants from southern and eastern Europe and barred Asians completely. The quota did not pertain to North Americans, however.

Harding's policies, his genial nature, and the return of prosperity made the president extremely popular. His sudden death, of a cerebral embolism, in the summer of 1923 resulted in a national outpouring of grief. Yet it soon became evident that his administration had been the most corrupt since that of Ulysses S. Grant. Harding had appointed venal mediocrities, many of them old cronies, to office, and they had betrayed his trust. The most publicized scandal was the illegal leasing of naval oil reserves at Teapot Dome, Wyo., which led to the conviction of Secretary of the Interior Albert B. Fall for accepting a bribe.

Calvin Coolidge, Harding's vice president and successor, was a taciturn,

Document: Thomas J. Walsh: Teapot Dome (1924)

In 1921 Albert B. Fall, newly appointed secretary of the interior, obtained jurisdiction for his department over certain oil fields in Wyoming and California that had previously been administered by the Navy Department. Fall made arrangements with two private companies to extract the oil, in return for financial favours for himself. It seems likely that President Harding knew most of the facts of the case before his death in August 1923, for members of Congress had already begun to ask questions and suggestive articles had been printed in newspapers. But the full scope of the scandal—each of the oil companies stood to gain more than $100 million, and Fall could anticipate a fortune for himself—was not made public until an investigation was undertaken by Montana Sen. Thomas J. Walsh. In July 1924 Walsh published an article, part of which is reprinted here, outlining the background of the case. The leases were canceled in 1927; two years later Fall was fined $100,000 and sent to prison.

Our government is operated on the party system. That system has its vices, but one of its cardinal virtues is that the one party, always standing ready to point out the objections to and the weaknesses of candidates, officials, policies, and measures of the other, better men are advanced as candidates, officials are held to a higher degree of efficiency, and a stricter responsibility and policies demanded by the public interest are pursued. So it is no discredit whatever to either me or my colleagues, if it be the fact, as has been so acrimoniously charged, that no sense of public duty, no detestation of crime, no love of country actuated us, that our activities are and have been, as charged, "pure politics."

With both friends and foes, however, there is an acute curiosity to know the sequence of events which ended in the public disgrace of Fall, by what sinuous and devious route the pursuit which led to his exposure was followed, and to learn of the intellectual processes by which that result was achieved. It is a queer trait of human character that finds gratification in the reading of detective stories. This tale reveals some queer manifestations of the operations of the mass mind....

Albert B. Fall, U.S. secretary of the interior under Pres. Warren G. Harding, was the first American to be convicted of a felony committed while holding a Cabinet post. © Everett Collection/SuperStock

parsimonious Vermont Yankee who restored honesty to government. His administration suffered none of the stigma of the Harding scandals, and Coolidge, thanks to a buoyant economy and a divided Democratic Party, easily defeated the conservative Democrat John W. Davis in the election of 1924. Even though an independent campaign by Sen. Robert M. La Follette of Wisconsin drew off insurgent Republicans, Coolidge received more popular, and electoral, votes than his opponents combined.

Coolidge followed Harding's policies, and prosperity continued for most of the decade. From 1922 to 1929, stock dividends rose by 108 percent, corporate profits by 76 percent, and wages by 33 percent. In 1929, 4,455,100 passenger cars were sold by American factories, one for every 27 members of the population, a record that was not broken until 1950. Productivity was the key to America's economic growth. Because of improvements in technology, overall labour costs declined by nearly 10 percent, even though the wages of individual workers rose.

The prosperity of the United States in the 1920s was not solidly based, however. The wealthy benefited most, and

Document: Calvin Coolidge: The Destiny of America (1923)

In 1923, while serving as vice president, Calvin Coolidge gave a Memorial Day Address in the simple, homespun language which typified all of his future utterances. In discussing the destiny of America, the thrifty, conservative Coolidge, who was almost puritanical in his zeal for old-fashioned virtues, reiterated the familiar myths in so persuasive a way that some people believed, one historian has said, that they were hearing them for the first time. A portion of the speech is reprinted here.

Patriotism is easy to understand in America. It means looking out for yourself by looking out for your country. In no other nation on earth does this principle have such complete application. It comes most naturally from the fundamental doctrine of our land that the people are supreme. Lincoln stated the substance of the whole matter in his famous phrase, "government of the people; by the people, and for the people."

The authority of law here is not something which is imposed upon the people; it is the will of the people themselves. The decision of the court here is not something which is apart from the people; it is the judgment of the people themselves. The right of the ownership of property here is not something withheld from the people; it is the privilege of the people themselves. Their sovereignty is absolute and complete. A definition of the relationship between the institutions of our government and the American people entirely justifies the assertion that: "All things were made by them; and without them was not anything made that was made." It is because the American government is the sole creation and possession of the people that they have always cherished it and defended it, and always will....

agriculture and several industries, such as textiles and bituminous coal mining, were seriously depressed; after 1926 construction declined.

NEW SOCIAL TRENDS

For millions of Americans, the sober-minded Coolidge was a more appropriate symbol for the era than the journalistic terms Jazz Age or Roaring Twenties. These terms were exaggerations, but they did have some basis in fact. Many young men and women who had been disillusioned by their experiences in World War I rebelled against what they viewed as unsuccessful, outmoded prewar conventions and attitudes. Women who had been forced to work outside the home because of labour shortages during the war were unwilling to give up their social and economic independence after the war had ended. Having won the right to vote when the Nineteenth Amendment was ratified in 1920, the new "emancipated" woman, the flapper, demanded to be recognized as man's equal in all areas. She adopted a masculine look, bobbing her hair and abandoning corsets; she drank and smoked in public; and she was more open about sex.

Social changes were not limited to women and the young. Productivity gains brought most Americans up to at least a modest level of comfort. People were working fewer hours a week and earning more money than ever before. New consumer goods—radios, telephones, refrigerators, and above all the motor car—made life

Two young women dressed in the flapper style of the day walk hand in hand along the beach in Atlantic City, N.J., c. 1924. © Underwood Photo Archives/SuperStock

better, and they were easier to buy thanks to a vastly expanded consumer credit system. Leisure activities became more important, professional sports boomed, and the rapid growth of tabloid newspapers, magazines, movies, and radios enabled millions to share in the exciting world of speakeasies, flappers, and jazz music, even if only vicariously.

On the darker side, antiforeign sentiment led to the revival of the racist, anti-Semitic, and anti-Catholic Ku Klux Klan, especially in rural areas. During the early 1920s the Klan achieved a membership of some 5,000,000 and gained

Nineteenth Amendment

Opposition to woman suffrage in the United States predated the Constitutional Convention (1787), which drafted and adopted the Constitution. The prevailing view within society was that women should be precluded from holding office and voting—indeed, it was generally accepted (among men) that women should be protected from the evils of politics. Still, there was opposition to such patriarchal views from the beginning, as when Abigail Adams, wife of John Adams, asked her husband in 1776, as he went to the Continental Congress to adopt the Declaration of Independence, to "remember the ladies and be more generous and favourable to them than your ancestors." In the scattered places where women could vote in some types of local elections, they began to lose this right in the late 18th century.

From the founding of the United States, women had been almost universally excluded from voting and their voices largely suppressed from the political sphere. Beginning in the early 19th century, as women chafed at these restrictions, the movement for woman suffrage began and was tied in large part to agitation against slavery. In July 1848 in Seneca Falls, N.Y., then the hometown of Elizabeth Cady Stanton, the Seneca Falls Convention launched the women's rights movement and also called for woman suffrage. The Civil War (1861-65) resulted in the end of the institution of slavery, and in its aftermath many women abolitionists put on hold their desire for universal suffrage in favour of ensuring suffrage for newly freed male slaves.

Gradually throughout the second half of the 19th century, certain states and territories extended often limited voting rights to women. Wyoming Territory granted women the right to vote in all elections in 1869. But it soon became apparent that an amendment to the federal Constitution would be a preferable plan for suffragists. Two organizations were formed in 1869: the National Woman Suffrage Association, which sought to achieve a federal constitutional amendment that would secure the ballot for women; and the American Woman Suffrage Association, which focused on obtaining amendments to that effect in the constitutions of the various states. The two organizations worked together closely and would merge in 1890.

In 1878 a constitutional amendment was introduced in Congress that would enshrine woman suffrage for all elections. It would be reintroduced in every Congress thereafter. In 1890 Wyoming became a state and thus also became the first state whose constitution guaranteed women the right to vote. Over the next decade several other states—all in the western part of the country—joined Wyoming. In 1912, when then former Pres. Theodore Roosevelt ran (unsuccessfully) as a third-party candidate for president, his party became the first national party to adopt a plank supporting a constitutional amendment.

In January 1918, with momentum clearly behind the suffragists—15 states had extended equal voting rights to women, and the amendment was formally supported by both parties and by Pres. Woodrow Wilson—the amendment passed with the bare minimum two-thirds support in the House of Representatives, but it failed narrowly in the U.S. Senate. This galvanized the National Woman's Party, which led a campaign seeking to oust senators who had voted against it.

THE AWAKENING

Titled The Awakening, *this 1915 illustration by Henry Mayer shows a torch-bearing woman labelled "Votes for Women" striding across the western states—where women already had the right to vote—toward the east where women are reaching out to her in their awakening desire for suffrage.* Library of Congress Prints and Photographs Division

A subsequent attempt to pass the amendment came in 1919, and this time it passed both chambers with the requisite two-thirds majority—304-89 in the House of Representatives on May 21, and 56-25 in the Senate on June 4. Although the amendment's fate seemed in doubt, because of opposition throughout much of the South, on Aug. 18, 1920, Tennessee—by one vote—became the 36th state to ratify the amendment, thereby ensuring its adoption. On August 26 the Nineteenth Amendment was proclaimed by the secretary of state as being part of the Constitution of the United States.

The full text of the amendment is:

The right of citizens of the United States to vote shall not be denied or abridged by the United States or by any State on account of sex.

Congress shall have power to enforce this article by appropriate legislation.

control of, or influence over, many city and state governments. Rural areas also provided the base for a Christian fundamentalist movement, as farmers and small-town dwellers who felt threatened and alienated by the rapidly expanding, socially changing cities fought to preserve American moral standards by stressing religious orthodoxy.

The fundamentalist movement grew steadily until 1925, when John T. Scopes, a high-school biology teacher in Dayton, Tenn., was tried for violating a law common to many Southern states prohibiting the teaching of any doctrine denying the divine creation of man as taught by the Bible, including Charles Darwin's theory of evolution. World attention focused on the highly publicized trial (later known as the "Monkey Trial"), which promised confrontation between fundamentalist literal belief and liberal interpretation of the Scriptures. William Jennings Bryan led for the prosecution and Clarence Darrow for

Document: Harry Emerson Fosdick: The Fundamentalist Controversy (1922)

As the American Protestant churches tried desperately to adjust to the rapid social, economic, and political changes of the early 20th century, a rift developed between those who felt a need for a new "social gospel" and those who would accept only the literal truths of the Bible. In 1909 12 small pamphlets titled The Fundamentals laid the groundwork for the movement called fundamentalism by delineating what was felt to be the necessary beliefs of Christianity, while denouncing such ideas as Darwinism and all forms of evolutionary socialism. By the early 1920s the "modernist-fundamentalist" controversy was well under way. In 1922 the noted preacher Harry Emerson Fosdick analyzed—and criticized—the fundamentalist position in a sermon from which the following selection is taken.

This morning we are to think of the Fundamentalist controversy which threatens to divide the American churches as though already they were not sufficiently split and riven. A scene, suggestive for our thought, is depicted in the fifth chapter of the Book of the Acts, where the Jewish leaders hale before them Peter and other of the apostles because they had been preaching Jesus as the Messiah. Moreover, the Jewish leaders propose to slay them, when in opposition Gamaliel speaks: "Refrain from these men, and let them alone; for if this counsel or this work be of men, it will be overthrown; but if it is of God ye will not be able to overthrow them; lest haply ye be found even to be fighting against God." ...

Already all of us must have heard about the people who call themselves the Fundamentalists. Their apparent intention is to drive out of the evangelical churches men and women of liberal opinions. I speak of them the more freely because there are no two denominations more affected by them than the Baptist and the Presbyterian. We should not identify the Fundamentalists with the conservatives. All Fundamentalists are conservatives, but not all conservatives are Fundamentalists. The best conservatives can often give lessons to the liberals in true liberality of spirit, but the Fundamentalist program is essentially illiberal and intolerant....

Antievolution books on sale in Dayton, Tenn., 1925, where the trial of high-school biology teacher John T. Scopes took place. Topical Press Agency/Hulton Archive/Getty Images

the defense. The judge ruled out any test of the law's constitutionality or argument on the validity of the theory, limiting the trial to the single question of whether Scopes had taught evolution, which he admittedly had. He was convicted and fined $100. (On appeal, the state Supreme Court upheld the constitutionality of the 1925 law but acquitted Scopes on the technicality that he had been fined excessively.) Although Scopes was found guilty, both the law itself and fundamentalist beliefs were ridiculed during the course of the trial.

One fundamentalist goal that was achieved was the passage in 1919 of the Prohibition (Eighteenth) Amendment, which prohibited the manufacture, sale, or transportation of intoxicating liquors. Millions of mostly Protestant churchgoers hailed Prohibition as a moral advance, and the liquor consumption of working people, as well as the incidence of alcohol-related diseases and deaths, does seem to have dropped during the period. On the other hand, millions of otherwise law-abiding citizens drank the prohibited liquor, prompting the growth of organized crime. The illegal liquor business was so lucrative and federal prohibition enforcement machinery was so slight that gangsters were soon engaged in the large-scale smuggling, manufacture, and sale of alcoholic beverages.

As in legitimate business, the highest profits came from achieving economies of scale, so gangsters engaged in complex mergers and takeovers; but, unlike corporate warfare, the underworld used real guns to wipe out competition. In 1931 a national law-enforcement commission, formed to study the flouting of prohibition and the activities of gangsters, was to report that prohibition was virtually unenforceable; and, with the coming of the Great Depression, prohibition ceased to be a key political issue. In 1933 the Twenty-first Amendment brought its repeal.

In the meantime, prohibition and religion were the major issues of the 1928 presidential campaign between the Republican nominee, Herbert Hoover, and the Democrat, Gov. Alfred E. Smith of New York. Smith was an opponent of prohibition and a Roman Catholic. His candidacy brought enthusiasm and a heavy Democratic vote in the large cities, but a landslide against him in the dry and Protestant hinterlands secured the election for Hoover.

Federal authorities resorted to a variety of techniques in their efforts to crack down on illegal liquor being sold during Prohibition, as evidenced by these before and after photographs showing two agents headed for a speakeasy, c. 1925. Underwood and Underwood/Time & Life Pictures/ Getty Images

Eighteenth Amendment

The Eighteenth Amendment emerged from the organized efforts of the temperance movement and Anti-Saloon League, which attributed to alcohol virtually all of society's ills and led campaigns at the local, state, and national levels to combat its manufacture, sale, distribution, and consumption. Most of the organized efforts supporting prohibition involved religious coalitions that linked alcohol to immorality, criminality, and, with the advent of World War I, unpatriotic citizenship. The amendment passed both chambers of the U.S. Congress in December 1917 and was ratified by the requisite three-fourths of the states in January 1919. Its language called for Congress to pass enforcement legislation, and this was championed by Andrew Volstead, chairman of the House Judiciary Committee, who engineered passage of the National Prohibition Act (commonly referred to as the Volstead Act). The act was conceived by Anti-Saloon League leader Wayne Wheeler and passed over the veto of Pres. Woodrow Wilson.

Neither the Volstead Act nor the Amendment was enforced with great success. Indeed, entire illegal economies (bootlegging, speakeasies, and distilling operations) flourished. The public appetite for alcohol remained and was only intensified with the stock market crash of 1929. In March

In a show of near-athletic bartending at Sloppy Joe's Bar in Chicago, 1933, the repeal of the 18th Amendment is celebrated. American Stock/Archive Photos/Getty Images

1933, shortly after taking office, Pres. Franklin D. Roosevelt signed the Cullen-Harrison Act, which amended the Volstead Act, permitting the manufacturing and sale of low-alcohol beer and wines (up to 3.2 percent alcohol by volume). Nine months later, on Dec. 5, 1933, federal prohibition was repealed with the ratification of the Twenty-first Amendment (which allowed prohibition to be maintained at the state and local levels). The Eighteenth Amendment is the only amendment to have secured ratification and later been repealed.

The full text of the Amendment is:

Section 1—After one year from the ratification of this article the manufacture, sale, or transportation of intoxicating liquors within, the importation thereof into, or the exportation thereof from the United States and all territory subject to the jurisdiction thereof for beverage purposes is hereby prohibited.

Section 2—The Congress and the several States shall have concurrent power to enforce this article by appropriate legislation.

Section 3—This article shall be inoperative unless it shall have been ratified as an amendment to the Constitution by the legislatures of the several States, as provided in the Constitution, within seven years from the date of the submission hereof to the States by the Congress.

CHAPTER 2

THE GREAT DEPRESSION

No decade in the 20th century was more terrifying for people throughout the world than the 1930s. The traumas of the decade included economic disorder, the rise of totalitarianism, and the coming (or presence) of war. Nevertheless, the decade is remembered in different ways in different parts of the world. For people in the United States, the 1930s was indelibly the age of the Great Depression.

Having left Iowa in 1932 and seen here along a highway in New Mexico in 1936, this impoverished family is about to sell its trailer and belongings to raise cash for food. Library of Congress Prints and Photographs Division

THE STOCK MARKET CRASH

In October 1929, only months after Hoover took office, the stock market crashed, the average value of 50 leading stocks falling by almost half in two months. During the mid- to late 1920s, the stock market had undergone rapid expansion. It continued for the first six months following Hoover's inauguration in January 1929. The prices of stocks soared to fantastic heights in the great "Hoover bull market," and the public, from banking and industrial magnates to chauffeurs and cooks, rushed to brokers to invest their surplus or their savings in securities, which they could sell at a profit. Billions of dollars were drawn from the banks into Wall Street for brokers' loans to carry margin accounts. The spectacles of the South Sea Bubble (speculation mania that ruined many British investors in 1720) and the Mississippi Bubble (a financial scheme in 18th-century France that triggered a speculative frenzy and ended in financial collapse) had returned. People sold their Liberty Bonds and mortgaged their homes to pour their cash into the stock market. In the midsummer of 1929 some 300 million shares of stock were being carried on margin, pushing the Dow Jones Industrial Average to a peak of 381 points in September. Any warnings of the precarious foundations of this financial house of cards went unheeded.

Prices began to decline in September and early October, but speculation continued, fueled in many cases by individuals who had borrowed money to buy shares—a practice that could be sustained only as long as stock prices continued rising. (When the market tumbled, those who had bought stocks on margin not only lost the value of their investment, they also owed money to the entities that had granted the loans for stock purchases.) On October 18 the market went into a free fall, and the wild rush to buy stocks gave way to an equally wild rush to sell. The first day of real panic, October 24, is known as Black Thursday; on that day a record 12.9 million shares were traded as investors rushed to salvage their losses. Still, the Dow average closed down only six points after a number of major banks and investment companies bought up great blocks of stock in a successful effort to stem the panic that day. Their attempts, however, ultimately failed to shore up the market.

The panic began again on Black Monday (October 28), with the market closing down 12.8 percent. On Black Tuesday (October 29) more than 16 million shares were traded. The Dow Jones Industrial Average lost another 12 percent and closed at 198—a drop of 183 points in less than two months. Prime securities tumbled like the issues of bogus gold mines. General Electric fell from 396 on September 3 to 210 on October 29. American Telephone and Telegraph (AT&T) dropped 100 points. DuPont fell from a summer high of 217 to 80, United States Steel from 261 to 166, Delaware and Hudson from 224 to 141, and Radio Corporation of America (RCA) common stock from 505 to 26. Political

Headline of the Brooklyn Daily Eagle, *Oct. 24, 1929, announcing the news of Wall Street's tumbling stocks.* Icon Communications/Archive Photos/Getty Images

and financial leaders at first affected to treat the matter as a mere spasm in the market, vying with one another in reassuring statements. President Hoover and Treasury Secretary Andrew W. Mellon led the way with optimistic predictions that business was "fundamentally sound" and that a great revival of prosperity was "just around the corner." Although the Dow Jones Industrial Average nearly reached the 300 mark again in 1930, it sank rapidly in May 1930.

In addition to rampant speculation, other factors likely contributed to the collapse of the stock market. Among the more prominent causes were tightening of credit by the Federal Reserve (in August 1929 the discount rate was raised from 5 percent to 6 percent), the proliferation of holding companies and investment trusts (which tended to create debt), a multitude of large bank loans that could not be liquidated, and an economic recession that had begun earlier in the summer. Despite occasional rallies, the slide persisted until 1932, when stock averages were barely a fourth of what they had been in 1929. Industrial production soon followed the stock market, giving rise to the worst unemployment the country had ever seen. By 1933 at least a quarter of the work force was unemployed. Adjusted for deflation, salaries had fallen by 40 percent and industrial wages by 60 percent.

THE DUST BOWL

The causes of the Great Depression were many and various. Agriculture had collapsed in 1919 and was a continuing source of weakness. This was especially true in the Great Plains, where large portions of southeastern Colorado, southwestern Kansas, the panhandles of Texas and Oklahoma, and northeastern New Mexico became known as the Dust Bowl in the early 1930s. The area's grasslands had supported mostly stockraising until World War I, when millions of acres were put under the plow in order to grow wheat. Following years of overcultivation and generally poor land management in the 1920s, the region—which receives an average rainfall of less than 20 inches in a typical year—suffered a severe drought in the early 1930s that lasted several years. The area's exposed topsoil, robbed of the anchoring, water-retaining roots of its native grasses, was carried off by heavy spring winds. "Black blizzards" of windblown soil blocked out the sun and piled the dirt in drifts. Occasionally the dust storms swept completely across the country to the East Coast. Thousands of families were forced to leave the region at the height of the Great Depression in the early and mid-1930s.

John Steinbeck's *The Grapes of Wrath* (1939), the most illustrious of the "protest" novels of the Great Depression era, was an epic tribute to the Okies (Oklahomans displaced by the Dust Bowl), throwbacks to America's 19th-century pioneers who were run off their farms by the banks, clattering in their trucks and jalopies across the Arizona desert on Route 66 to the advertised promised land in California, a despised caste of migrant labourers. But the Great Plains were not the only part of the country where the rural way of life was marginalized. Hard times came elsewhere, most notably in South.

Photojournalist Arthur Rothstein's iconic photograph of the American Dust Bowl shows a father and his sons walking toward a shack in Oklahoma during a dust storm, 1936. Library of Congress Prints and Photographs Division

Document: Report on Conditions in the South (1938)

The National Emergency Council's report on economic conditions in the South, transmitted on July 25, 1938, was initially undertaken because of Pres. Franklin D. Roosevelt's conviction that the South presented the country with its most serious economic problem. The highly documented report bore out his suspicion but evoked widespread criticism. Reprinted here are four of the report's 15 sections; the first describes the region's soil.

Nature gave the South good soil. With less than a third of the nation's area, the South contains more than a third of the nation's good farming acreage. It has two-thirds of all the land in America receiving a forty-inch annual rainfall or better. It has nearly half of the land on which crops can grow for six months without danger of frost.

This heritage has been sadly exploited. Sixty-one percent of all the nation's land badly damaged by erosion is in the Southern states. An expanse of Southern farmland as large as South Carolina has been gullied and washed away; at least 22 million acres of once fertile soil has been ruined beyond repair. Another area the size of Oklahoma and Alabama combined has been seriously damaged by erosion. In addition, the sterile sand and gravel washed off this land has covered over a fertile valley acreage equal in size to Maryland.

There are a number of reasons for this wastage:

Much of the South's land originally was so fertile that it produced crops for many years no matter how carelessly it was farmed. For generations thousands of Southern farmers plowed their furrows up and down the slopes, so that each furrow served as a ditch to hasten the runoff of silt-laden water after every rain. While many farmers have now learned the importance of terracing their land or plowing it on the contours, thousands still follow the destructive practice of the past....

THE DEPRESSION GOES GLOBAL

Because of poor regulatory policies, many banks were overextended. Wages had not kept up with profits, and by the late 1920s consumers were reaching the limits of their ability to borrow and spend. Production had already begun to decline and unemployment to rise before the crash. The crash, which was inevitable since stock prices were much in excess of real value, greatly accelerated every bad tendency, destroying the confidence of investors and consumers alike.

Hoover met the crisis energetically, in contrast to earlier administrations, which had done little to cope with panics except reduce government spending. He extracted promises from manufacturers to maintain production. He signed legislation providing generous additional sums for public works. He also signed the infamous Smoot–Hawley Tariff of 1930, which raised duties to an average level of 50 percent. These steps failed to ease the depression, however, while the tariff helped to export it. International trade had never recovered from World War I. Europe still depended on American sales and investments for income and on American loans to maintain the complicated structure of debt payments and reparations erected in the 1920s. After the crash Americans stopped investing in Europe, and the tariff deprived foreigners of their American markets. Foreign nations struck back with tariffs of their own, and all suffered from the resulting anarchy.

In the 1930 elections the Democratic Party won control of the House of Representatives and, in combination with liberal Republicans, the Senate as well. Soon afterward a slight rise in production and employment made it seem that the worst of the depression was over. Then, in the spring of 1931, another crisis erupted. The weakening western European economy brought down a major bank in Vienna, and Germany defaulted on its WWI reparations payments. Hoover proposed a one-year moratorium on reparations and war-debt payments, but, even though the moratorium was adopted, it was too little too late. In the resulting financial panic most European governments went off the gold standard and devalued their currencies, thus destroying the exchange system, with devastating effects upon trade.

Europeans withdrew gold from American banks, leading the banks to call in their loans to American businesses. A cascade of bankruptcies ensued, bank customers collapsing first and after them the banks.

Hoover tried hard to stabilize the economy. He persuaded Congress to establish a Reconstruction Finance Corporation to lend funds to banks, railroads, insurance companies, and other institutions. At the same time, in January 1932, new capital was arranged for federal land banks. The Glass–Steagall Act provided gold to meet foreign withdrawals and liberalized Federal Reserve credit. The Federal Home

The Gold Standard

The gold standard is the name for a monetary system in which the standard unit of currency is a fixed weight of gold or—if gold money is not used—the currency is kept at the value of a fixed weight of gold. In an internal gold standard, gold coins circulate as legal tender, or paper money is freely convertible to gold at a fixed price.

In an international gold standard system, gold or a currency that is convertible into gold at a fixed price is used as a means of making international payments. Exchange rates between countries are fixed. If these rates rise or fall by more than the cost of shipping gold from one country to another, large inflows or outflows of gold occur until the rates are stabilized. The gold standard was first put into operation in Great Britain in 1821. The full international gold standard lasted from about 1870 until World War I.

The abandonment of the gold standard and the resultant fluctuating gold prices served as encouragement for many people to sell their gold possessions. Here, a shop assistant weighs gold articles for one such man, c. 1932. Topical Press Agency/Hulton Archive/Getty Images

Loan Bank Act sought to prop up threatened building and loan associations. But these measures failed to promote recovery or to arrest the rising tide of unemployment. Hoover, whose administrative abilities had masked severe political shortcomings, made things worse by offering negative leadership to the country. His public addresses were conspicuously lacking in candor. He vetoed measures for direct federal relief, despite the fact that local governments and private charities, the traditional sources for welfare, were clearly incapable of providing adequate aid for the ever-rising numbers of homeless and hungry. When unemployed veterans refused to leave Washington after their request for immediate payment of approved bonuses was denied, Hoover sent out the army, which dispersed the protesters at bayonet point and burned down their makeshift quarters.

Hoover's failures and mistakes guaranteed that whoever the Democrats nominated in 1932 would become the next president. Their candidate was Gov. Franklin Delano Roosevelt of New York. He won the election by a large margin, and the Democrats won majorities in both branches of Congress.

CHAPTER 3

THE FIRST NEW DEAL

Franklin D. Roosevelt took office amid a terrifying bank crisis that had forced many states to suspend banking activities. He acted quickly to restore public confidence. On Inaugural Day, March 4, 1933, he declared that "the only thing we have to fear is fear itself." The next day he halted trading in gold and declared a national "bank holiday." On March 9 he submitted to Congress an Emergency Banking Bill authorizing government to strengthen, reorganize, and reopen solvent banks. The House passed the bill by acclamation, sight unseen, after only 38 minutes of debate. That night the Senate passed it unamended, 73 votes to 7. On March 12 Roosevelt announced that, on the following day, sound banks would begin to reopen. On March 13, deposits exceeded withdrawals in the first reopened banks. "Capitalism was saved in eight days," Raymond Moley, a member of the president's famous "brain trust," later observed.

In fact, the legal basis for the bank holiday was doubtful. The term itself was a misnomer, intended to give a festive air to what was actually a desperate last resort. Most of the reopened banks were not audited to establish their solvency; instead the public was asked to trust the president.

Herbert Hoover and Franklin Delano Roosevelt being driven to the U.S. Capitol for Roosevelt's inauguration as the 32nd president of the United States, March 4, 1933. Library of Congress Prints and Photographs Division

Nevertheless, the bank holiday exemplified brilliant leadership at work. It restored confidence where all had been lost and saved the financial system. Roosevelt followed it up with legislation that did actually put the banking structure on a solid footing. The Glass–Steagall Act of 1933 separated commercial from investment banking and created the Federal Deposit Insurance Corporation to guarantee small deposits. The Banking Act of 1935 strengthened the Federal Reserve System, the first major improvement since its birth in 1913.

With the country enthusiastically behind him, Roosevelt kept Congress in special session and piece by piece sent it recommendations that formed the basic recovery program of his first 100 days in office. From March 9 to June 16, 1933, Congress enacted all of Roosevelt's proposals.

Document: Franklin D. Roosevelt: Progress of the Recovery Program (1933)

In addition to his regular news conferences with the press, Roosevelt kept the American people informed of public policy by radio in what came to be known as Fireside Chats. He regarded these broadcasts as instruments of public education in national affairs as well as a way of enlisting support for his program. The following selection is the third of the Fireside Chats and was delivered July 24, 1933, to sum up the legislation of the "Hundred Days" and to launch the Blue Eagle program. This endeavour, under the supervision of Hugh S. Johnson, head of the National Recovery Administration (NRA), was designed to enlist popular support for the NRA and to get as many businesses as possible

President Roosevelt as pictured on the cover of Collier's magazine, 1941. Courtesy Franklin D. Roosevelt Library

involved in its cooperative program; cooperating stores and businesses displayed the Blue Eagle emblem.

For many years the two great barriers to a normal prosperity have been low farm prices and the creeping paralysis of unemployment. These factors have cut the purchasing power of the country in half. I promised action. Congress did its part when it passed the Farm and the Industrial Recovery acts. Today we are putting these two acts to work and they will work if people understand their plain objectives.

First, the Farm Act: It is based on the fact that the purchasing power of nearly half our population depends on adequate prices for farm products. We have been producing more of some crops than we consume or can sell in a depressed world market. The cure is not to produce so much. Without our help the farmers cannot get together and cut production, and the Farm Bill gives them a method of bringing their production down to a reasonable level and of obtaining reasonable prices for their crops. I have clearly stated that this method is in a sense experimental, but so far as we have gone we have reason to believe that it will produce good results....

Among the bills Congress passed was one creating the Tennessee Valley Authority, which would build dams and power plants and in many other ways salvage a vast, impoverished region. The Securities Exchange Act gave the Federal Trade Commission broad new regulatory powers, which in 1934 were passed on to the newly created Securities and Exchange Commission. The Home Owners Loan Act established a corporation that refinanced one of every five mortgages on urban private residences. Other bills passed during the Hundred Days, as well as subsequent legislation, provided aid for the unemployed and the working poor and attacked the problems of agriculture and business.

RELIEF

Nothing required more urgent attention than the masses of unemployed workers who, with their families, had soon overwhelmed the miserably underfinanced bodies that provided direct relief. On May 12, 1933, Congress established a Federal Emergency Relief Administration to distribute half a billion dollars to state and local agencies. Roosevelt also created the Civil Works Administration, which by January 1934 was employing more than 4,000,000 men and women. Alarmed by rising costs, Roosevelt dismantled the CWA in 1934, but the persistence of high unemployment led him to make another about-face.

In 1935 the Emergency Relief Appropriation Act provided almost $5,000,000,000 to create work for some 3,500,000 persons. The Public Works Administration (PWA), established in 1933, provided jobs on long-term construction projects, and the Civilian Conservation Corps put 2,500,000 young men to work planting or otherwise

Document: Franklin D. Roosevelt: Relief, Recovery, and Reform (1934)

The economy reached its low point in the summer of 1933 and thereafter showed signs of recovering. Between 1933 and 1934 national income rose by about 25 percent and employment increased by more than 2,500,000. In June 1934 Roosevelt told Congress that the emergency of the Depression had been met and that government could now turn to charting long-term reforms. Roosevelt reviewed the year past and presented a prospectus for the future in the first Fireside Chat of 1934, broadcast to the country on June 28.

It has been several months since I have talked with you concerning the problems of government. Since January, those of us in whom you have vested responsibility have been engaged in the fulfillment of plans and policies which had been widely discussed in previous months. It seemed to us our duty not only to make the right path clear, but also to tread that path.

As we review the achievements of this session of the Seventy-third Congress, it is made increasingly clear that its task was essentially that of completing and fortifying the work it had begun in March 1933. That was no easy task, but the Congress was equal to it. It has been well said that while there were a few exceptions, this Congress displayed a greater freedom from mere partisanship than any other peacetime Congress since the administration of President Washington himself. The session was distinguished by the extent and variety of legislation enacted and by the intelligence and goodwill of debate upon these measures....

Men heading for newfound work, courtesy of the Civilian Conservation Corps (CCC), c. 1935. CCC work projects, which were primarily geared for young unmarried men, included planting trees, building flood barriers, fighting forest fires, and maintaining forest roads and trails. PhotoQuest/Archive Photos/Getty Images

improving huge tracts of forestland. For homeowners, the Federal Housing Administration began insuring private home-improvement loans to middle-income families in 1934; in 1938 it became a home-building agency as well.

AGRICULTURAL RECOVERY

Hoover's Federal Farm Board had tried to end the long-standing agricultural depression by raising prices without limiting production. Roosevelt's Agricultural Adjustment Act (AAA) of 1933 was designed to correct the imbalance. Farmers who agreed to limit production would receive "parity" payments to balance prices between farm and nonfarm products, based on prewar income levels.

Farmers benefited also from numerous other measures, such as the Farm Credit Act of 1933, which refinanced a fifth of all farm mortgages in a period of 18 months, and the creation in 1935 of the Rural Electrification Administration (REA), which did more to bring farmers into the 20th century than any other single act. Thanks to the REA, nine out of 10

Doucment: Henry A. Wallace: Declaration of Interdependence (1933)

On May 10, 1933, Congress passed the Agricultural Adjustment Act, which sought to restore the balance between the agricultural and industrial sectors of the economy by limiting farm production and relieving the burden of farm mortgages. On May 13 Secretary of Agriculture Henry A. Wallace went on the radio with what he called a declaration of interdependence to explain the administration's intent with regard to the new farm bill. A portion of his radio address is reprinted here.

The new Farm Act signed by President Roosevelt yesterday comprises twenty-six pages of legal document, but the essence of it can be stated simply. It has three main parts. The word "adjustment" covers all three.

First, the administration is empowered to adjust farm production to effective demand as a means of restoring the farmer's purchasing power. The secretary of agriculture is charged to administer this adjustment and to direct, at the same time, an effort to reduce those wastes of distribution which now cause food to pile up, unused, while people go hungry a hundred miles away.

Second is an accompanying authorization to refinance and readjust farm mortgage payments. ...

In the third part of the act, the power for controlled inflation is delegated to the President, and this too signifies adjustment — adjustment of currency and credit to our changed needs. My own responsibility, however, as secretary of agriculture is solely with the first part of the act.

It should be made plain at the outset that the new Farm Act initiates a program for a general advance in buying power, and advance that must extend throughout America, lightening the way of the people in city and country alike. We must lift urban buying power as we lift farm prices. The Farm Act must not be considered an isolated advance in a restricted sector; it is an important part of a large-scale, coordinated attack on the whole problem of depression....

farms were electrified by 1950, compared to one out of 10 in 1935.

These additional measures were made all the more important by the limited success of the AAA. Production did fall as intended, aided by the severe drought of 1933–36, and prices rose in consequence; but many, perhaps a majority, of farmers did not prosper as a result. The AAA was of more value to big operators than to small family farmers, who often could not meet their expenses if they restricted their output and therefore could not qualify for parity payments. The farm corporation, however, was able to slash its labour costs by cutting acreage and could cut costs further by using government subsidies to purchase machinery. Thus, even before the Supreme Court invalidated the AAA in 1936, support for it had diminished.

BUSINESS RECOVERY

As the economic crisis was above all an industrial depression, business recovery headed the New Deal's list of priorities. Working toward that goal, the administration drafted the National Industrial Recovery Act of 1933, which, among other things, created a National Recovery Administration to help business leaders draw up and enforce codes governing prices, wages, and other matters (coded industries would be exempt from the antitrust laws). Labour was offered protection from unfair practices and given the right to bargain collectively. A large-scale public works appropriation, administered through the PWA, was intended to pour sufficient money into the economy to increase consumer buying power while prices and wages went up.

Despite great initial enthusiasm for the NRA program, it was a failure. The codes became too numerous and complex for proper enforcement, and they were resented because they tended to favour the leading producers in each regulated industry. The protections afforded labour proved illusory, while the PWA, despite an impressive building record that included not only dams, bridges, and schools but also aircraft carriers, was too slow and too small to have much effect on the economy as a whole.

Yet, even if the NRA had overcome its technical problems, failure would probably still have resulted. What the country needed was economic growth, but the NRA assumed that the United States had a mature economic structure incapable of further expansion. Accordingly, it worked to stabilize the economy, eliminate wasteful or predatory competition, and protect the rights of labour. Encouraging growth was not on its agenda.

The doomed National Recovery Administration—lampooned here in a 1935 cartoon show-ing Pres. Franklin D. Roosevelt trying to save a drowning Uncle Sam from the rising tide of the depression—met its end when the Supreme Court invalidated it in 1935. Stock Montage/ Archive Photos/Getty Images

CHAPTER 4

THE SECOND NEW DEAL

In reaction to pressures from the left and hostility from the right, the New Deal shifted more toward reform in 1935–36. Popular leaders, promising more than Roosevelt, threatened to pull sufficient votes from him in the 1936 election to bring Republican victory.

POPULIST CHALLENGERS

Of the several demagogues who attained a national following during the depression, Huey P. Long ("Kingfish")—who came to power as the governor of Louisiana—was the most ambitious, the most fascinating, and the most deeply feared. As a United States senator in 1932 he formulated a "Share-the-Wealth" program to save America.

The poor in Northern cities were attracted to the Roman Catholic priest Charles E. Coughlin, who later switched from a program of nationalization and currency inflation to an anti-Democratic, anti-Semitic emphasis. Many older people supported Francis E. Townsend's plan to provide $200 per month for everyone over age 60. At the same time, conservatives, including such groups as the American Liberty League,

Document: Huey P. Long: Sharing Our Wealth (1935)

In 1934 Sen. Huey P. Long converted his "Share-the-Wealth" ("Every Man a King") program into a national crusade by establishing the Share-Our-Wealth Society and inviting Americans everywhere to organize local branches. The Society, he prophesied, would eventually displace the two major political parties and then elevate him to the presidency. The description of Long's program below is taken from a radio address given by him in January 1935. At the height of his power, Long was shot by an assassin, the son-in-law of a judge Long had vilified, in the capitol building at Baton Rouge, La., on Sept. 8, 1935.

President Roosevelt was elected on Nov. 8, 1932. People look upon an elected President as the President. This is January 1935. We are in our third year of the Roosevelt depression, with the conditions growing worse. ...

We must now become awakened! We must know the truth and speak the truth. There is no use to wait three more years. It is not Roosevelt or ruin; it is Roosevelt's ruin.

Now, my friends, it makes no difference who is President or who is senator. America is for 125 million people and the unborn to come. We ran Mr. Roosevelt for the presidency of the United States because he promised to us by word of mouth and in writing:

- That the size of the big man's fortune would be reduced so as to give the masses at the bottom enough to wipe out all poverty; and
- That the hours of labor would be so reduced that all would share in the work to be done and in consuming the abundance mankind produced.

Hundreds of words were used by Mr. Roosevelt to make these promises to the people, but they were made over and over again. He reiterated these pledges even after he took his oath as President. Summed up, what these promises meant was: "Share our wealth."...

Huey Long giving a speech, c. 1930s.
Fotosearch/Archive Photos/Getty Images

founded in 1934, attacked the New Deal as a threat to states' rights, free enterprise, and the open shop.

THE WORKS PROGRESS ADMINISTRATION

Roosevelt's response in 1935 was to propose greater aid to the underprivileged and extensive reforms. Congress created the Works Progress Administration, which replaced direct relief with work relief; between 1935 and 1941 the WPA employed an annual average of 2,100,000 workers, including artists and writers, who built or improved schools, hospitals, airports, and other facilities by the tens of thousands. The National Youth Administration created part-time jobs for millions of college students, high-school students, and other youngsters.

The New Deal rationale for the Federal Art Project, the Federal Music Project, the Federal Writers' Project, and the Federal Theatre Project as part of the WPA was that—just like construction workers—writers, musicians, painters, and actors had to eat. It was also important that they use their skills for the benefit of society. Consequently, the Federal Theatre Project performances were staged not on Broadway but in working-class and African American neighbourhoods, outside factory gates, and in small towns whose residents had never seen a play. The Federal Writers' Project arranged for thousands of interviews with blue-collar workers, small farmers, fishermen, miners, lumberjacks, waitresses, and former slaves, and it published guidebooks that explored the history, ethnic composition, folklore, and ecology of every state. The Federal Music

Works Progress Administration poster created by artist Vera Bock. Showing a farmer and a labourer shaking hands, the poster reinforces the "WPA brand" by also having the acronym stand for Work Pays America. Fotosearch/Archive Photos/Getty Images

Project sponsored free concerts and the musical transcription of half-forgotten sea chanteys, cowboy and folk songs, Indian dances, Quaker hymns, and black spirituals. The Federal Art Project funded art education, established art centres, and made it possible for thousands of artists to complete works in sculpture, painting, and graphic arts; in addition, the Public Works of Art Project, influenced by Mexican painters such as José Clemente Orozco and Diego Rivera, arranged for murals to be painted on the walls of post offices and county courthouses depicting the stories of particular regions and local communities. It was precisely this attraction to traditional American melodies and to Norman Rockwell-like illustrations of ordinary life that helped composers such as Aaron Copland and Virgil Thomson and painters such as Thomas Hart Benton and Ben Shahn, all of them trained in the European modernist aesthetics of Stravinsky or Picasso, to adapt avant-garde techniques to "American" themes and hence offer an art accessible to popular taste.

THE SOCIAL SECURITY ACT, THE WAGNER ACT, AND THE SUPREME COURT

Of long-range significance was the Social Security Act of 1935, which provided federal aid for the aged, retirement annuities, unemployment insurance, aid for persons who were blind or disabled, and aid to dependent children; the original act suffered from various inadequacies, but it was the beginning of a permanent, expanding national program.

A tax reform law fell heavily upon corporations and well-to-do people. The National Labor Relations Act, or Wagner Act, gave organized labour federal protection in collective bargaining; it prohibited a number of "unfair practices" on the part of employers and created the strong National Labor Relations Board to enforce the law.

In the 1936 elections Roosevelt, aided by his reform program, formed a coalition that included liberals, urban ethnics, farmers, trade unionists, and the elderly. He easily defeated the Republican nominee for president, Gov. Alfred ("Alf") M. Landon of Kansas, receiving more

President Roosevelt signing the Social Security Act, Aug. 14, 1935. FPG/Archive Photos/Getty Images

Document: Franklin D. Roosevelt: A Program for Social Security (1935)

Presidential advisers spent much of 1934 considering programs for unemployment compensation and old-age benefits—important planks in the Democratic platform of 1932. Unemployment compensation created numerous problems, largely because of conflict between advocates of a national plan and proponents of state-operated plans. Old-age insurance, having had no precedent in state legislation, was generally deemed suitable for a uniform federal program. In the following message to Congress of Jan. 17, 1935, Roosevelt presented the administration's proposal for a Social Security act. A bill was finally passed on August 14. Like most of the New Deal legislation, Social Security was challenged as unconstitutional, but in May 1937 the Supreme Court upheld the major provisions of the law.

In addressing you on June 8, 1934, I summarized the main objectives of our American program. Among these was, and is, the security of the men, women, and children of the nation against certain hazards and vicissitudes of life. This purpose is an essential part of our task. In my annual message to you I promised to submit a definite program of action. This I do in the form of a report to me by a Committee on Economic Security, appointed by me for the purpose of surveying the field and of recommending the basis of legislation.

I am gratified with the work of this committee and of those who have helped it: The Technical Board of Economic Security, drawn from various departments of the government; the Advisory Council on Economic Security, consisting of informed and public-spirited private citizens; and a number of other advisory groups, including a Committee on Actuarial Consultants, a Medical Advisory Board, a Dental Advisory Committee, a Hospital Advisory Committee, a Public Health Advisory Committee, a Child Welfare Committee, and an Advisory Committee on Employment Relief. All of those who participated in this notable task of planning this major legislative proposal are ready and willing at any time to consult with and assist in any way the appropriate congressional committees and members with respect to detailed aspects....

than 60 percent of the popular vote and the electoral votes of every state except Maine and Vermont. The Democratic majorities in the House and Senate were also strengthened. Viewing his decisive victory as an electoral mandate for continued reform, Roosevelt sought to neutralize the Supreme Court, which in 1935 had invalidated several early New Deal reform measures and now seemed about to strike down the Wagner Act and the Social Security Act. In February 1937 Roosevelt created a furor by proposing a reorganization of the court system that would have included giving him the power to appoint up to six new justices, thus giving the court a liberal majority. Some Democrats and a few liberal Republicans in Congress supported the proposal, but a strong coalition of Republicans and conservative Democrats, backed by much public support, fought the so-called court-packing plan.

Meanwhile the court itself in a new series of decisions began upholding as constitutional measures involving both state and federal economic regulation. These decisions, which began an extensive revision of constitutional law concerning governmental regulation, made the reorganization plan unnecessary; the Senate defeated it in July 1937 by a vote of 70 to 22. Roosevelt had suffered a stinging political defeat, even though he no longer had to fear the court. Turnover on the court was rapid as older members retired or died; by 1942 all but two of the justices were Roosevelt appointees.

THE CULMINATION OF THE NEW DEAL

Roosevelt lost further prestige in the summer of 1937, when the country plunged into a sharp recession. Economists had feared an inflationary boom as industrial production moved up to within 7.5 percent of 1929. Other indices were high except for a lag in capital investment and continued heavy unemployment. Roosevelt, fearing a boom and eager to balance the budget, cut government spending, which most economists felt had brought the recovery. The new Social Security taxes removed an additional $2,000,000,000 from circulation. Between August 1937 and May 1938 the index of production fell from 117 to 76 (on a 1929 base of 100), and unemployment increased by perhaps 4,000,000 persons. Congress voted an emergency appropriation of $5,000,000,000 for work relief and public works, and by June 1938 recovery once more was under way, although unemployment remained higher than before the recession.

Roosevelt's loss of power became evident in 1938, when his attempts to defeat conservative congressional Democrats in the primaries failed. In the fall Republicans gained 80 seats in the House and seven in the Senate. The Democratic Party retained nominal control of Congress, but conservative Democrats

The Fair Labor Standards Act

Sponsored by Sen. Robert F. Wagner of New York, signed on June 14, 1938, and promulgated on Oct. 24, 1938, the Fair Labor Standards Act (also known as Wages and Hours Act) was the first act in the United States prescribing nationwide compulsory federal regulation of wages and hours. The law, applying to all industries engaged in interstate commerce, established a minimum wage of 25 cents per hour for the first year, to be increased to 40 cents within seven years. No worker was obliged to work, without compensation at overtime rates, more than 44 hours a week during the first year, 42 the second year, and 40 thereafter.

Created by artist and graphic designer Lester Beall, this U.S. Housing Authority poster depicts the hand of government replacing clapboard shacks with superior housing. Hulton Archive/ Getty Images

and Republicans voting together defeated many of Roosevelt's proposals. A few last bills slipped through. The U.S. Housing Authority was created in 1937 to provide low-cost public housing. In 1938 the Fair Labor Standards Act established a minimum wage and a maximum work week. Otherwise, the president seldom got what he asked for.

Apart from the New Deal itself, no development in the 1930s was more important than the rise of organized labour. This too had negative, or at least mixed, effects upon Roosevelt's political power. When the depression struck, only 5 percent of the work force was unionized, compared to 12 percent in 1920. The great change began in 1935 when the American Federation of Labor's Committee for Industrial Organization broke away from its timid parent and, as the Congress of Industrial Organizations , began unionizing the mass production industries.

The CIO had a unique tool, the sit-down strike. Instead of picketing a plant, CIO strikers closed it down from inside, taking the factory hostage and preventing management from operating with nonunion workers. This tactic, together with the new reluctance of authorities, many of them Roosevelt Democrats, to act against labour, made sit-down strikes highly successful. On Feb. 11, 1937, after a long sit-down strike, General Motors,

Document: John L. Lewis: Industrial Unions (1938)

The devotion of the American Federation of Labor (AFL) to the principle of craft unionism prevented it from becoming an effective organizer of industrial workers during the 1930s. When its 1935 convention failed to adopt a position favourable to this hitherto ignored segment of the American working class, John L. Lewis, along with Sidney Hillman, David Dubinsky, and Thomas McMahon, formed the Committee for Industrial Organization within the AFL. Continuing strife in the parent body, combined with highly successful membership drives by the Committee, led the latter to

American labour leader John L. Lewis advocated higher wages, improved working conditions, and the right of American work-ers to join unions. Thomas D. McAvoy/Time & Life Pictures/Getty Images

break with the AFL and to form the independent Congress of Industrial Organizations (CIO) in November 1938. Lewis, president of the United Mine Workers, was named chairman of the first convention of the Congress and addressed it in that capacity.

I profoundly appreciate the opportunity of opening this convention with greetings through President Fagan of organized labor in this great industrial section, with the greetings of His Honor, the mayor of Pittsburgh, extended in behalf of the people of this great municipality, with the greetings of the Christian churches, represented by the eminent clergymen who are present this morning, and the acclaim of our own people.

Why these greetings? Why this interest? Why this enthusiasm? Why this acclaim? Because there has been born in America a new, modern labor movement dedicated to the proposition that all who labor are entitled to equality of opportunity, the right to organize, the right to participate in the bounties and the blessings of this country and our government, the right to aspire to an equality of position, and the right to express views, objectives, and rights on a parity with any other citizen, whatever may be his place, his condition of servitude, or the degree of world's goods which he may possess.

So that is the greeting of the Committee for Industrial Organization, assembled here and about to formalize its own internal affairs and make permanent its form of organization....

Workers at General Motors' Chevrolet automobile plant in Flint, Mich., cross off the number of days they have been on a sit-down strike, Feb. 10, 1937. On the following day, GM would recognize the United Auto Workers as the bargaining agent for its employees. New York Daily News Archive/Getty Images

the country's mightiest corporation, recognized the United Auto Workers. The United States Steel Corporation caved in less than a month later, and by 1941 some 10,500,000 workers were unionized, three times as many as a decade before. The CIO became a mainstay of the New Deal coalition, yet it also aroused great resentment among middle-class Americans, who opposed strikes in general but the CIO's methods especially. This further narrowed Roosevelt's political base.

AN ASSESSMENT OF THE NEW DEAL

The New Deal established federal responsibility for the welfare of the economy and the American people. At the time, conservative critics charged it was bringing statism or even socialism. Left-wing critics of a later generation charged just the reverse—that it bolstered the old order and prevented significant reform. Others suggested that the New Deal was no more than the extension and culmination of progressivism. In its early stages, the New Deal did perhaps begin where progressivism left off and built upon the Hoover program for fighting the depression. But Roosevelt soon took the New Deal well beyond Hoover and progressivism, establishing a precedent for large-scale social programs and for government participation in economic activities. Despite the importance of this growth of federal responsibility, the New Deal's greatest achievement was to restore faith in American democracy at a time when many people believed that the only choice left was between communism and fascism. Its greatest failure was its inability to bring about complete economic recovery. Some economists, notably John Maynard Keynes, a British economist best known for his revolutionary theories on the causes of prolonged unemployment, were calling for massive deficit spending to promote recovery; and by 1937 the New Deal's own experience proved that pump priming worked, whereas spending cutbacks only hurt the economy. Roosevelt remained unpersuaded, however, and the depression lingered on until U.S. entry into World War II brought full employment.

CHAPTER 5

THE ROAD TO WAR

After World War I most Americans concluded that participating in international affairs had been a mistake. They sought peace through isolation and throughout the 1920s advocated a policy of disarmament and nonintervention. As a result, relations with Latin-American countries improved substantially under Hoover, an anti-imperialist. This enabled Roosevelt to establish what became known as the Good Neighbor Policy, which repudiated altogether the right of intervention in Latin America. By exercising restraint in the region as a whole and by withdrawing American occupation forces from the Caribbean, Roosevelt increased the prestige of the United States in Latin America to its highest level in memory.

As the European situation became more tense, the United States continued to hold to its isolationist policy. Congress, with the approval of Roosevelt and Secretary of State Cordell Hull, enacted a series of neutrality laws that legislated against the factors that supposedly had taken the United States into World War I. As Italy prepared to invade Ethiopia, Congress passed the Neutrality Act of 1935, embargoing shipment of arms to either aggressor or victim. Stronger legislation followed the outbreak of the Spanish Civil War in 1936, in effect

Federal Art Project poster created to help publicize Roosevelt's Good Neighbor Policy. Library of Congress Prints and Photographs Division

Document: Franklin D. Roosevelt: The Good Neighbor Policy (1936)

Three decades of strained relations with the Latin American countries were reversed during the Hoover administration, largely through the work of Secretary of State Henry L. Stimson. Roosevelt, who later named Stimson his secretary of war, resolved to continue the policy of not interfering in the internal affairs of Latin America and seeking alliances there. In an address at Chautauqua, N.Y., on Aug. 14, 1936, part of which is reprinted here, the president explained his "Good Neighbor Policy."

Long before I returned to Washington as President of the United States, I had made up my mind that, pending what might be called a more opportune moment on other continents, the United States could best serve the cause of a peaceful humanity by setting an example. That was why on the 4th of March, 1933, I made the following declaration:

In the field of world policy I would dedicate this nation to the policy of the good neighbor — the neighbor who resolutely respects himself and, because he does so, respects the rights of others — the neighbor who respects his obligations and respects the sanctity of his agreements in and with a world of neighbors.

This declaration represents my purpose; but it represents more than a purpose, for it stands for a practice. To a measurable degree it has succeeded; the whole world now knows that the United States cherishes no predatory ambitions. We are strong; but less powerful nations know that they need not fear our strength. We seek no conquest: we stand for peace....

penalizing the Spanish government, whose fascist enemies were receiving strong support from Italy's Benito Mussolini and Germany's Adolph Hitler.

In the Pacific Roosevelt continued Hoover's policy of nonrecognition of Japan's conquests in Asia. When Japan invaded China in 1937, however, Roosevelt seemed to begin moving away from isolationism. He did not invoke the Neutrality Act, which had just been revised, and in October he warned that war was like a disease and suggested that it might be desirable for peace-loving countries to "quarantine" aggressor countries. He then quickly denied that his statement had any policy implications, and by December, when Japanese aircraft sank a U.S. gunboat in the Yangtze River, thoughts of reprisal were stifled by public apathy and by Japan's offer of apologies and indemnities. With strong public opposition to foreign intervention, Roosevelt concentrated on regional defense, continuing to build up the navy and signing mutual security agreements with other governments in North and South America.

When Germany's invasion of Poland in 1939 touched off World War II,

Roosevelt called Congress into special session to revise the Neutrality Act to allow belligerents (in reality only Great Britain and France, both on the Allied side) to purchase munitions on a cash-and-carry basis. With the fall of France to Germany in June 1940, Roosevelt, with heavy public support, threw the resources of the United States behind the British. He ordered the War and Navy departments to resupply British divisions that had been rescued at Dunkirk minus their weaponry, and in September he agreed to exchange 50 obsolescent destroyers for 99-year leases on eight British naval and air bases in the Western Hemisphere.

The question of how much and what type of additional aid should be given to the Allies became a major issue of the election of 1940, in which Roosevelt ran for an unprecedented third term. Public opinion polls, a new influence upon decision makers, showed that most Americans favoured Britain but still wished to stay out of war. Roosevelt's opponent, Wendell Willkie, capitalized on this prevailing mood, and he rose steadily in the polls by attacking the president as a warmonger.

Document: Wendell L. Willkie: Acceptance Speech (1940)

The three leading Republican contenders for the presidency in 1940 were Sen. Robert A. Taft of Ohio, Sen. Arthur H. Vandenberg of Michigan, and Thomas Dewey, later governor of New York. Wendell Willkie, without a political organization and with little party support, was a dark horse. However, by the time the Republican Convention opened in June there was a rising tide for Willkie, and he was nominated on the sixth ballot. On August 17 Willkie delivered his acceptance speech, a portion of which is reprinted here, in his hometown of Elwood, Ind. In the election Willkie carried only 10 states, but he polled over 22 million votes, more than any previous Republican candidate.

Presidential candidate Wendell Willkie, photographed by John Phillips, on the cover of the weekly picture magazine, Life, Sept. 30, 1940. John Phillips/Time & Life Pictures/Getty Images

No man is so wise as to foresee what the future holds or to lay out a plan for it. No man can guarantee to maintain peace. Peace is not something that a nation can achieve by itself. It also depends on what some other country does. It is neither practical nor desirable to adopt a foreign program committing the United States to future action under unknown circumstances.

The best that we can do is to decide what principle shall guide us.

For me, that principle can be simply defined: In the foreign policy of the United States, as in its domestic policy, I would do everything to defend American democracy and I would refrain from doing anything that would injure it.

We must not permit our emotions — our sympathies or hatreds — to move us from that fixed principle.

For instance, we must not shirk the necessity of preparing our sons to take care of themselves in case the defense of America leads to war. I shall not undertake to analyze the legislation on this subject that is now before Congress, or to examine the intentions of the Administration with regard to it. I concur with many members of my party, that these intentions must be closely watched. Nevertheless, in spite of these considerations, I cannot ask the American people to put their faith in me without recording my conviction that some form of selective service is the only democratic way in which to secure the trained and competent manpower we need for national defense....

An alarmed Roosevelt fought back, going so far as to make what he knew was an empty promise. "Your boys," he said just before the election, "are not going to be sent into any foreign wars." In truth, both candidates realized that U.S. intervention in the war might become essential, contrary to their public statements. Roosevelt won a decisive victory.

Upon being returned to office, Roosevelt moved quickly to aid the Allies. His Lend-Lease Act, passed in March 1941 after vehement debate, committed the United States to supply the Allies on credit. When Germany, on March 25, extended its war zone to include Iceland and the Denmark Straits, Roosevelt retaliated in April by extending the American Neutrality Patrol to Iceland. In July the United States occupied Iceland, and U.S. naval vessels began escorting convoys of American and Icelandic ships. That summer Lend-Lease was extended to the Soviet Union after it was invaded by Germany. In August Roosevelt met with the British prime minister, Winston Churchill, off the coast of Newfoundland to issue a set of war aims known as the Atlantic Charter.

It called for national self-determination, larger economic opportunities, freedom from fear and want, freedom of the seas, and disarmament.

Although in retrospect U.S. entry into World War II seems inevitable, in 1941 it was still the subject of great debate. Isolationism was a strong political force, and many influential individuals were determined that U.S. aid policy stop short of war. In fact, as late as Aug. 12, 1941, the House of Representatives extended the Selective Training and Service Act of

Document: Franklin D. Roosevelt: The Four Freedoms (1941)

In his annual message to Congress on Jan. 6, 1941, President Roosevelt called upon Congress to enact the Lend-Lease program that he had first proposed at a press conference the previous December. Roosevelt's Lend-Lease program extended military supplies to Great Britain to aid it in its war against Nazi Germany. Though the first part of the message concerned itself with the war in Europe and sought to define America's war aims, the latter part was more significant as an expression of Roosevelt's vision of the future. Known as the Four Freedoms Speech, it was a formulation of the social and political goals that the president hoped to attain for the American people, as well as the people of the world, following the war.

Just as our national policy in internal affairs has been based upon a decent respect for the rights and dignity of all our fellow-men within our gates, so our national policy in foreign affairs has been based on a decent respect for the rights and dignity of all nations, large and small. And the justice of morality must and will win in the end.

Our national policy is this:

First, by an impressive expression of the public will and without regard to partisanship, we are committed to all-inclusive national defense.

Second, by an impressive expression of the public will and without regard to partisanship, we are committed to full support of all those resolute peoples, everywhere, who are resisting aggression and are thereby keeping war away from our Hemisphere. By this support, we express our determination that the democratic cause shall prevail, and we strengthen the defense and security of our own nation.

Third, by an impressive expression of the public will and without regard to partisanship, we are committed to the proposition that principles of morality and considerations for our own security will never permit us to acquiesce in a peace dictated by aggressors and sponsored by appeasers. We know that enduring peace cannot be bought at the cost of other people's freedom....

1940 by a vote of only 203 to 202. Despite isolationist resistance, Roosevelt pushed cautiously forward. In late August the navy added British and Allied ships to its Icelandic convoys. Its orders were to shoot German and Italian warships on sight, thus making the United States an undeclared participant in the Battle of the Atlantic. During October one U.S. destroyer was damaged by a German U-boat and another was sunk. The United States now embarked on an undeclared naval war against Germany, but Roosevelt refrained from asking for a formal declaration of war. According to public opinion polls, a majority of Americans still hoped to remain neutral.

The war question was soon resolved by events in the Pacific. As much as a distant neutral could, the United States had been supporting China in its war against Japan, yet it continued to sell

Document: The Atlantic Charter (1941)

From Aug. 9 to 12, 1941, President Roosevelt and British Prime Minister Churchill held a secret meeting on a ship off the coast of Newfoundland, the first of the conferences between the heads of the anti-Axis powers. At the conclusion of the conference they issued the Atlantic Charter, a declaration of Anglo-American goals for a better world, written largely by Churchill. Although that document, reproduced here, was neither a treaty nor a signed official paper but merely a press release, it nonetheless marked the beginning of the close cooperation between the United States and Britain that characterized the war years. The aims of the Atlantic Charter were later embodied in the Declaration of the United Nations in January 1942.

Source: 77 Congress, 1 Session, House Document No. 358.

Joint declaration of the President of the United States of America and the Prime Minister, Mr. Churchill, representing His Majesty's government in the United Kingdom, being met together, deem it right to make known certain common principles in the national policies of their respective countries on which they base their hopes for a better future for the world.

First, their countries seek no aggrandizement, territorial or other.

Pres. Franklin D. Roosevelt and British Prime Minister Winston Churchill aboard the HMS Prince of Wales in Placentia Bay, Newfoundland, August 1941. The result of the waterborne conference was the Atlantic Charter. Fox Photos/Hulton Archive/Getty Images

Second, they desire to see no territorial changes that do not accord with the freely expressed wishes of the peoples concerned.

Third, they respect the right of all peoples to choose the form of government under which they will live; and they wish to see sovereign rights and self-government restored to those who have been forcibly deprived of them.

Fourth, they will endeavor, with due respect for their existing obligations, to further the enjoyment by all states, great or small, victor or vanquished, of access, on equal terms, to the trade and to the raw materials of the world which are needed for their economic prosperity.

Fifth, they desire to bring about the fullest collaboration between all nations in the economic field with the object of securing, for all, improved labor standards, economic advancement, and social security.

Sixth, after the final destruction of the Nazi tyranny, they hope to see established a peace which will afford to all nations the means of dwelling in safety within their own boundaries, and which will afford assurance that all the men in all the lands may live out their lives in freedom from fear and want.

Seventh, such a peace should enable all men to traverse the high seas and oceans without hindrance.

Eighth, they believe that all of the nations of the world, for realistic as well as spiritual reasons, must come to the abandonment of the use of force. Since no future peace can be maintained if land, sea, or air armaments continue to be employed by nations which threaten, or may threaten, aggression outside of their frontiers, they believe, pending the establishment of a wider and permanent system of general security, that the disarmament of such nations is essential. They will likewise aid and encourage all other practicable measures which will lighten for peace-loving peoples the crushing burden of armaments.

Japan products and commodities essential to the Japanese war effort. Then, in July 1940, the United States applied an embargo on the sale of aviation gas, lubricants, and prime scrap metal to Japan. When Japanese armies invaded French Indochina in September with the apparent purpose of establishing bases for an attack on the East Indies, the United States struck back by embargoing all types of scrap iron and steel and by extending a loan to China. Japan promptly retaliated by signing a limited treaty of alliance, the Tripartite Pact, with Germany and Italy. Roosevelt extended a much larger loan to China and in December embargoed iron ore, pig iron, and a variety of other products.

Japan and the United States then entered into complex negotiations in the spring of 1941. Neither country would compromise on the China question, however, Japan refusing to withdraw and the United States insisting upon it. Believing that Japan intended to attack the East Indies, the United States stopped exporting oil to Japan at the end of the summer. In effect an ultimatum, since Japan had

A small boat coming to the rescue of crewmembers on the nearly 32-ton USS West Virginia, *Dec. 7, 1941, following the surprise aerial attack on Pearl Harbor. Smoke billows out where the most extensive damage occurred.* Library of Congress Prints and Photographs Division

limited oil stocks and no alternative source of supply, the oil embargo confirmed Japan's decision to eliminate the U.S. Pacific Fleet and to conquer Southeast Asia, thereby becoming self-sufficient in crude oil and other vital resources. By the end of November Roosevelt and his military advisers knew (through intercepted Japanese messages) that a military attack was likely; they expected it to be against the East Indies or the Philippines. To their astonishment, on December 7 Japan directed its first blow against naval and air installations in Hawaii. In a bold surprise

attack, Japanese aircraft destroyed or damaged 18 ships of war at Pearl Harbor, including the entire battleship force, and 347 planes. Total U.S. casualties amounted to 2,403 dead and 1,178 wounded.

On Dec. 8, 1941, Congress with only one dissenting vote declared war against Japan. Three days later Germany and Italy declared war against the United States; and Congress, voting unanimously, reciprocated. As a result of the attack on Pearl Harbor, the previously divided nation entered into the global struggle with virtual unanimity.

CHAPTER 6

THE UNITED STATES AT WAR

Although isolationism died at Pearl Harbor, its legacy of unpreparedness lived on. Anticipating war, Roosevelt and his advisers had been able to develop and execute some plans for military expansion, but public opinion prohibited large-scale appropriations for armament and defense. Thus, when Pearl Harbor was attacked, the United States had some 2,200,000 men under arms, but most were ill-trained and poorly equipped. Barely a handful of army divisions even approached a state of readiness. The Army Air Corps possessed only 1,100 combat planes, many of which were outdated. The navy was better prepared, but it was too small to fight a two-ocean war and had barely been able to provide enough ships for convoy duty in the North Atlantic. Eventually more than 15,000,000 men and women would serve in the armed forces, but not until 1943 would the United States be strong enough to undertake large-scale offensive operations.

WAR PRODUCTION

Roosevelt had begun establishing mobilization agencies in 1939, but none had sufficient power or authority to bring order out of the chaos generated as industry converted to war production. He therefore created the War Production Board in January 1942 to coordinate mobilization, and in 1943 an Office of War Mobilization was established to supervise the host of defense agencies that had sprung up in Washington, D.C. Gradually, a priorities system was devised to supply defense plants with raw materials; a synthetic rubber industry was developed from scratch; rationing conserved scarce resources; and the Office of Price Administration kept inflation under control.

After initial snarls and never-ending disputes, by the beginning of 1944 production was reaching astronomical totals—double those of all the enemy countries combined. Hailed at the time as a production miracle, this increase was about equal to what the country would have produced in peacetime, assuming full employment. War production might have risen even higher if regulation of civilian consumption and industry had been stricter.

Scientists, under the direction of the Office of Scientific Research and Development, played a more important role in production than in any previous war, making gains in rocketry, radar and sonar, and other areas. Among the new inventions was the proximity fuse, which contained a tiny radio that detonated an artillery shell in the vicinity of its target, making a direct hit unnecessary. Of greatest importance was the atomic bomb, developed by scientists in secrecy and first tested on July 6, 1945.

FINANCING THE WAR

The total cost of the war to the federal government between 1941 and 1945 was about $321,000,000,000 (10 times as much as World War I). Taxes paid 41 percent of the multi-billion dollar price tag, less than Roosevelt requested but more than the World War I figure of 33 percent. The remainder was financed by borrowing from financial institutions, an expensive method but one that Congress preferred over the alternatives of raising taxes even higher or making war bond purchases compulsory. In consequence the national debt increased fivefold, amounting to $259,000,000,000 in 1945. The Revenue Act of 1942 revolutionized the tax structure by increasing the number who paid income taxes from 13,000,000 to 50,000,000. At the same time, through taxes on excess profits and other sources of income, the rich were made to bear a larger part of the burden, making this the only period in modern history when wealth was significantly redistributed.

SOCIAL CONSEQUENCES OF THE WAR

Despite the vast number of men and women in uniform, civilian employment rose from 46,000,000 in 1940 to more than 53,000,000 in 1945. The pool of unemployed men dried up in 1943, and further employment increases consisted of women, minorities, and over- or underage males. These were not enough to

Document: Franklin D. Roosevelt: Discrimination in Wartime Employment (1941)

During the spring of 1941, leaders of the African American community laid plans for a march on Washington, D.C., on July 1. A. Philip Randolph, president of the Brotherhood of Sleeping Car Porters and one of the most influential African American leaders of the 20th century, explained the reasons for the march, which in fact did not occur. "When the defense program began and billions of the taxpayers' money were appropriated for guns, ships, tanks, and bombs," Randolph later said, "Negroes presented themselves for work only to be given the cold shoulder.... Not until their wrath and indignation took the form of a proposed protest march on Washington...did things begin to move in the form of defense jobs for Negroes." The march was averted by Roosevelt's Executive Order No. 8802, issued June 25, which established the President's Committee on Fair Employment Practices.

A. Philip Randolph addressing a meeting of the Brotherhood of Sleeping Car Porters, c. 1937. Rex Hardy Jr./Time & Life Pictures/Getty Images

Source: U.S. Congressional Service, 77 Congress, 1 Session, No. 8802.

Reaffirming policy of full participation in the defense program by all persons, regardless of race, creed, color, or national origin, and directing certain action in furtherance of said policy

Whereas it is the policy of the United States to encourage full participation in the national defense program by all citizens of the United States, regardless of race, creed, color, or national origin, in the firm belief that the democratic way of life within the nation can be defended successfully only with the help and support of all groups within its borders; and

Whereas there is evidence that available and needed workers have been barred from employment in industries engaged in defense production solely because of considerations of race, creed, color, or national origin to the detriment of workers' morale and of national unity:

Now, Therefore, by virtue of the authority vested in me by the Constitution and the statutes, and as a prerequisite to the successful conduct of our national defense production effort, I do hereby reaffirm the policy of the United States that there shall be no discrimination in the employment of workers in defense industries or government because of race, creed, color, or national origin; and I do hereby declare that it is the duty of employers and of labor organizations, in furtherance of said policy and of this order, to provide for the full and equitable participation of all workers in defense industries, without discrimination because of race, creed, color, or national origin;

And it is hereby ordered as follows:

- All departments and agencies of the government of the United States concerned with vocational and training programs for defense production shall take special measures appropriate to assure that such programs are administered without discrimination because of race, creed, color, or national origin.
- All contracting agencies of the government of the United States shall include in all defense contracts hereafter negotiated by them a provision obligating the contractor not to discriminate against any worker because of race, creed, color, or national origin.
- There is established in the Office of Production Management a Committee on Fair Employment Practice, which shall consist of a chairman and four other members to be appointed by the President. The chairman and members of the committee shall serve as such without compensation but shall be entitled to actual and necessary transportation, subsistence, and other expenses incidental to performance of their duties. The committee shall receive and investigate complaints of discrimination in violation of the provisions of this order and shall take appropriate steps to redress grievances which it finds to be valid. The committee shall also recommend to the several departments and agencies of the government of the United States and to the President all measures which may be deemed by it necessary or proper to effectuate the provisions of this order.

meet all needs, and by the end of the year a manpower shortage had developed.

One result of this shortage was that African Americans made significant social and economic progress. Although the armed forces continued to practice segregation, as did Red Cross blood banks, Roosevelt, under pressure from African Americans, who were outraged by the refusal of defense industries to integrate their labour forces, signed Executive Order 8802 on June 25, 1941.

Executive Order 8802 prohibited racial discrimination in job training programs and by defense contractors and established a Fair Employment Practices Committee to insure compliance. By the end of 1944 nearly 2,000,000 African Americans were at work in defense industries. As black contributions to the military and industry increased, so did their demands for equality. This sometimes led to racial hostilities, as on June 20, 1943, when mobs of whites invaded a predominantly African American section of Detroit. Nevertheless, the gains offset the losses. Lynching virtually died out, several states outlawed discriminatory

A storefront window acts as a message board for the Hastings Street Riot Information Bureau Citizens Committee, a group created by African Americans following the violent race riots in their section of Detroit. Gordon Coster/Time & Life Pictures/Getty Images

voting practices, and others adopted fair employment laws.

Full employment also resulted in raised income levels, which, through a mixture of price and wage controls, were kept ahead of inflation. Despite both this increase in income and a no-strike pledge given by trade union leaders after Pearl Harbor, there were numerous labour actions. Workers resented wage ceilings because much of their increased income went to pay taxes and was earned by working overtime rather than through higher hourly rates. In consequence, there were almost 15,000 labour stoppages during the war at a cost of some 36,000,000 man-days. Strikes were greatly resented, particularly by the armed forces, but their effects were more symbolic than harmful. The time lost amounted to only one-ninth of 1 percent of all hours worked.

Because Pearl Harbor had united the nation, few people were prosecuted for disloyalty or sedition, unlike during World

Document: Hugo Black, Felix Frankfurter, Frank Murphy, and Robert H. Jackson: *Korematsu* v. *United States* (1944)

After the attack on Pearl Harbor, U.S. government officials began to fear a Japanese invasion of the West Coast and, short of that, the possibility of sabotage and subversion by Japanese Americans living in the area. Though most of the Japanese immigrants were by then American citizens, and though some of them had been born in the United States, the War Department prevailed on President Roosevelt to relocate the Japanese Americans to special detention camps, where they stayed throughout the war. In 1943 the Supreme Court upheld the constitutionality of the government's policy, and in Korematsu v. United States, *a case decided in 1944, it reaffirmed its earlier decision. Parts of the Court's ruling, a concurring opinion, and two strong dissents are reprinted here.*

Mr. Justice Black delivered the opinion of the Court.

The petitioner, an American citizen of Japanese descent, was convicted in a Federal District Court for remaining in San Leandro, California, a "Military Area," contrary to Civilian Exclusion Order No. 34 of the Commanding General of the Western Command, U. S. Army, which directed that after May 9, 1942, all persons of Japanese ancestry should be excluded from that area. No question was raised as to petitioner's loyalty to the United States. The Circuit Court of Appeals affirmed, and the importance of the constitutional question involved caused us to grant certiorari.

It should be noted, to begin with, that all legal restrictions which curtail the civil rights of a single racial group are immediately suspect. That is not to say that all such restrictions are unconstitutional. It is to say that courts must subject them to the most rigid scrutiny. Pressing public necessity may sometimes justify the existence of such restrictions; racial antagonism never can.

In the instant case, prosecution of the petitioner was begun by information charging violation of an Act of Congress, of March 21, 1942, 56 Stat. 173, which provides that:

Whoever shall enter, remain in, leave, or commit any act in any military area or military zone prescribed, under the authority of an executive order of the President, by the secretary of war, or by any military commander designated by the secretary of war, contrary to the restrictions applicable to any such area or zone or contrary to the order of the secretary of war or any such military commander, shall, if it appears that he knew or should have known of the existence and extent of the restrictions or order and that his act was in violation thereof, be guilty of a misdemeanor and upon conviction shall be liable to a fine of not to exceed $5,000 or to imprisonment for not more than one year, or both, for each offense....

War I. The one glaring exception to this policy was the scandalous treatment of Japanese and Americans of Japanese descent. In 1942, on the basis of groundless racial fears and suspicions, virtually the entire Japanese-American population of the West Coast, amounting to 110,000 persons, was rounded up and imprisoned in "relocation" centres, which the inmates regarded as concentration camps.

More than 110,000 Americans of Japanese ancestry—including this little girl seen awaiting evacuation to a detention centre—were confined in internment camps for the duration of World War II. Dorothea Lange/Time & Life Pictures/Getty Images

Japanese-Americans lost their liberty, and in most cases their property as well, despite the fact that the Federal Bureau of Investigation, which had already arrested those individuals it considered security risks, had verified their loyalty.

THE 1944 ELECTION

Roosevelt soundly defeated Gov. Thomas E. Dewey of New York in the 1944 election, but his margin of victory was smaller than it had been previously. His running mate, chosen by party leaders who disliked former vice president Henry A. Wallace for his extreme liberalism, was Sen. Harry S. Truman of Missouri, a party Democrat who had distinguished himself by investigating fraud and waste among war contractors.

Harry S. Truman, c. 1940. Stock Montage/Archive Photos/Getty Images

CHAPTER 7

THE NEW U.S. ROLE IN WORLD AFFAIRS

The U.S. entry into World War II had brought an end to isolation, and President Roosevelt was determined to prevent a retreat into isolationism once the war was over. After a series of conferences in December 1941, Roosevelt and Prime Minister Churchill announced the formation of the United Nations, a wartime alliance of 26 nations. In 1943 Roosevelt began planning the organization of a post-war United Nations, meeting with congressional leaders to assure bipartisan support. The public supported Roosevelt's efforts, and that fall Congress passed resolutions committing the United States to membership in an international body "with power adequate to establish and to maintain a just and lasting peace." Finally, in the spring of 1945, delegates from 50 nations signed the charter for a permanent United Nations. In addition to political harmony, Roosevelt promoted economic cooperation, and, with his full support, in 1944 the World Bank and the International Monetary Fund were created to bar a return of the cutthroat economic nationalism that had prevailed before the war.

Throughout the war Roosevelt met with Churchill and Soviet leader Joseph Stalin to plan military strategy and

Document: The Yalta Agreement (1945)

The scene of the famous Yalta Conference of Feb. 4-11, 1945, was the summer palace of Czar Nicholas II on the Black Sea coast of the ravaged Crimea, only recently liberated from the Germans. The last meeting of the "Big Three" Allied leaders—Franklin Roosevelt, Winston Churchill, and Joseph Stalin—opened as victory in Europe was imminent. Roosevelt had been advised by the Joint Chiefs of Staff that Japan was capable of continued resistance and that Soviet participation in the Pacific war would save a million American casualties. The major questions to be resolved were—besides Soviet aid in the war against Japan—the partition of Germany, the future of the liberated nations of eastern Europe, and the establishment of an international organization to keep the peace. The most heated discussion revolved around the future of Poland, by then almost wholly occupied by the Red Army, but the question uppermost in Roosevelt's mind was probably the creation of a peace-keeping organization. Both Roosevelt and Churchill came to the conference firmly convinced that Soviet cooperation was essential, not only for ending the war quickly but also for the future success of the United Nations. The Yalta Agreement, reproduced here, was signed on February 11.

(From left) *Winston Churchill, Franklin Roosevelt, and Joseph Stalin at the Yalta Conference, 1945.* Universal Images Group/ Getty Images

- That a United Nations Conference on the proposed world organization should be summoned for Wednesday, 25 April, 1945, and should be held in the United States of America.
- The nations to be invited to this conference should be:
- (a) the United Nations as they existed on the 8 February, 1945, and
(b) such of the Associated Nations as have declared war on the common enemy by 1 March, 1945. (For this purpose by the term "Associated Nation" was meant the eight Associated Nations and Turkey.) When the Conference on World Organization is held, the delegates of the United Kingdom and United States of America will support a proposal to admit to original membership two Soviet Socialist republics, i.e., the Ukraine and White Russia.
- That the United States government on behalf of the Three Powers should consult the government of China and the French Provisional Government in regard to the decisions taken at the present conference concerning the proposed world organization.
- That the text of the invitation to be issued to all the nations which would take part in the United Nations Conference should be as follows....

On Aug. 9, 1945, three days after detonating a uranium-fueled atomic bomb over Hiroshima, Japan, the United States dropped a plutonium-fueled atomic bomb over the Japanese port of Nagasaki. Apic/Hulton Archive/Getty Images

postwar policy. His last great conference with them took place at Yalta in the Crimea in February 1945.

There policies were agreed upon to enforce the unconditional surrender of Germany, to divide it into zones for occupation and policing by the respective Allied forces, and to provide democratic regimes in eastern European nations. A series of secret agreements were also made at Yalta; chief among these was the Soviet pledge to enter the war against Japan after the German surrender, in return for concessions in East Asia.

Roosevelt died suddenly of a cerebral hemorrhage on April 12 and was succeeded by Truman. In the following months the German armed forces collapsed, and on May 7 all German forces surrendered. In the Pacific the invasions of Iwo Jima and Okinawa in early 1945 brought Japan under a state of siege. In the summer, before an invasion could take place, the United States dropped atomic bombs on Hiroshima and Nagasaki. On September 2 the surrender of Japan was signed in Tokyo harbour on the battleship *Missouri*.

Document: Harry S. Truman: Announcement of the Dropping of an Atomic Bomb on Hiroshima (1945)

The leaders of the Allied powers met at Potsdam, Ger., from July 17 to Aug. 2, 1945, to consider the fate of defeated Germany and to plan the final campaign against Japan. The U.S. representative was President Truman, who had succeeded to the presidency on Roosevelt's death three months before; Clement Attlee replaced Churchill as British prime minister during the course of the conference. The first declaration issued by the conferees was the "unconditional surrender" ultimatum presented to Japan on July 26. Earlier in the conference Truman had informed Churchill that the United States had successfully tested an atomic device on July 16, to which Churchill is supposed to have responded: "This is the Second Coming, in wrath." On July 25, a day before the ultimatum, Truman ordered the 20th Air Force at Saipan to use one of the two atomic bombs in their possession at the first opportunity after August 3 if Japan had not yet surrendered. On July 29 the Japanese cabinet decided to make no immediate comment on the ultimatum, but press reports of their decision indicated to Truman and the Joint Chiefs of Staff that they had "ignored" it. This note of apparent defiance, which may actually have been unintended, led to the decision in Washington to use the bombs. The first was dropped on Hiroshima on the morning of August 6, destroying over four square miles of the city and killing or injuring more than 135,000 people. The president's address to the country on August 6 is reprinted here.

Sixteen hours ago an American airplane dropped one bomb on Hiroshima, an important Japanese Army base. That bomb had more power than 20,000 tons of TNT. It had more than 2,000 times the blast power of the British "Grand Slam," which is the largest bomb ever yet used in the history of warfare.

The Japanese began the war from the air at Pearl Harbor. They have been repaid manyfold. And the end is not yet. With this bomb we have now added a new and revolutionary increase in destruction to supplement the growing power of our armed forces. In their present from these bombs are now in production, and even more powerful forms are in development.

It is an atomic bomb. It is a harnessing of the basic power of the universe. The force from which the sun draws its power has been loosed against those who brought war to the Far East.

Before 1939, it was the accepted belief of scientists that it was theoretically possible to release atomic energy. But no one knew any practical method of doing it. By 1942, however, we knew that the Germans were working feverishly to find a way to add atomic energy to the other engines of war with which they hoped to enslave the world. But they failed. We may be grateful to Providence that the Germans got the V-1's and V-2's late and in limited quantities and even more grateful that they did not get the atomic bomb at all.

CONCLUSION

Having survived the Great Crash, the Great Depression, and an immensely destructive war between the world's great powers, the United States emerged from the eventful quarter-century between 1920 and 1945 with a political, military, and economic might so extreme it needed a new word to describe it: superpower, a title it shared only with the Soviet Union. World War II had devastated Germany, Japan, and Italy. France had not been its own master for nearly five years of occupation, and Britain and its empire, exhausted by the conflict, had become less "great." On the other hand, despite the massive loss of life by America's "Greatest Generation" in combat, the United States was reinvigorated by World War II, ever stronger because the war had stoked the machinery of the American economy in ways that even the best-laid plans of the New Deal could not.

The growing pains of the American colossus, however, had also been extreme. The buoyant economy of the 1920s, which had seemed permanently on the rise, bottomed out spectacularly, taking most of the world's leading economies down with it. The ruined stock marketeer, leaping from an office window, became a powerful symbol for American capitalism on the brink of destruction. The topsoil of much of the country's bread basket simply blew away, scattering dreams and sowing a decade's worth of despair and desolation. Yet the United States survived, due in no small part to the steady, hopeful guidance of one of the country's most influential presidents, Franklin D. Roosevelt. Today, Roosevelt remains a controversial figure, revered by some and reviled by others for the same changes to the American way of life he helped institute. However one feels about Roosevelt, his impact was undeniable. With the end of the war, the stage was set for a period of tremendous prosperity and global influence for the country, but with it would come new questions regarding the role of the United States in the world and inequities within American society.

APPENDICES (DOCUMENTS)

ROBERT BENCHLEY: "THE MAKING OF A RED" (1919)

Source: *Nation*, March 15, 1919.

You couldn't have asked for anyone more regular than Peters. He was an eminently safe citizen. Although not rich himself, he never chafed under the realization that there were others who possessed great wealth. In fact, the thought gave him rather a comfortable feeling. Furthermore, he was one of the charter members of the war. Long before President Wilson saw the light, Peters was advocating the abolition of German from the public-school curriculum. There was, therefore, absolutely nothing in his record which would in the slightest degree alter the true blue of a patriotic litmus. And he considered himself a liberal when he admitted that there might be something in this man Gompers, after all. That is how safe he was.

But one night he made a slip. It was ever so tiny a slip, but in comparison with it De Maupassant's famous piece of string was barren of consequences. Shortly before the United States entered the war, Peters made a speech at a meeting of the Civic League in his home town. His subject was: "Inter-urban Highways: Their Development in the Past and Their Possibilities for the Future." So far, 100 percent American. But, in the course of his talk, he happened to mention the fact that war, as an institution, has almost always had an injurious effect on public improvements of all kinds. In fact (and note this well — the government's sleuth in the audience did) he said that, all other things being equal, if he were given his choice of war or peace in the abstract, he would choose peace as a condition under which to live. Then he went on to discuss the comparative values of macadam and wood blocks for paving.

In the audience was a civilian representative of the Military Intelligence Service. He had a premonition that some sort of attempt was going to be made at this meeting of the Civic League to discredit the war and America's imminent participation therein. And he was not disappointed (no Military Intelligence sleuth ever is), for in the remark of Peters, derogatory to war as an institution, his sharp ear detected the accent of the Wilhelmstrasse.

Time went by. The United States entered the war, and Peters bought Liberty Bonds. He didn't join the Army, it is true, but, then, neither did James M. Beck, and it is an open secret that Mr. Beck was for the war. Peters did what a few slangy persons called "his bit," and not without a certain amount of pride. But he did not hear the slow, grinding noise from that district in which are located the mills of the gods. He did not even know that there was an investigation going on in Washington to determine the uses to which German propaganda money had been put. That is, he didn't know it until he opened his newspaper one morning and, with that uncanny precipitation with which a man's eye lights on his own name, discovered that he had been mentioned in the dispatches. At first he thought that it might be an honor list of Liberty Bond holders, but a glance at the headline chilled that young hope in his breast. It read as follows:

PRO-GERMAN LIST BARED BY ARMY SLEUTH

Prominent Obstructionists Named at Senate Probe

And then came the list. Peters' eye ran instinctively down to the place where, in what seemed to him to be 24-point Gothic caps, was blazoned the name "Horace W. Peters, Pacifist Lecturer, Matriculated at Germantown (Pa.) Military School." Above his name was that of Emma Goldman, "Anarchist." Below came that of Fritz von Papen, "agent of the Imperial German Government in America," and Jeremiah O'Leary, "Irish and Pro-German Agitator."

Peters was stunned. He telegraphed to his senator at Washington and demanded that the outrageous libel be retracted. He telegraphed to the Military Intelligence office and demanded to know who was the slanderer who had traduced him, and who in h —— l this Captain Whatsisname was who had submitted the report. He telegraphed to Secretary Baker and he cabled to the President. And he was informed, by return stagecoach, that his telegrams had been received and would be brought to the attention of the addressees at the earliest possible moment.

Then he went out to look up some of his friends, to explain that there had been a terrible mistake somewhere. But he was coolly received. No one could afford to be seen talking with him after what had happened. His partner merely said: "Bad business, Horace. Bad business!" The elevator starter pointed him out to a subordinate, and Peters heard him explain: "That's Peters, Horace W. Peters. Did'je see his name in the papers this morning with them other German spies?" At the club, little groups of his friends dissolved awkwardly when they saw him approaching, and, after distant nods, disappeared in an aimless manner. After all, you could hardly blame them.

The next morning the Tribune had a double-leaded editorial entitled "Oatmeal," in which it was stated that the disclosures in Washington were revealing the most insidious of all kinds of German propaganda—that disseminated by supposedly respectable American citizens. "It is not a tangible propaganda. It is an emotional propaganda. To the unwary it may resemble real-estate news, or perhaps a patriotic song, but it is the pap of Prussianism. As an example, we need go no further than Horace W. Peters. Mr. Peters' hobby was interurban highways. A very pretty hobby, Mr. Peters, but it won't do. It won't do." The Times ran an editorial saying, somewhere in the midst of a solid slab of type, that no doubt it would soon be found that Mr. Peters nourished Bolshevist sentiments, along with his teammate Emma Goldman. Emma Goldman! How Peters hated that woman! He had once written a letter to this very paper about her, advocating her electrocution.

He dashed out again in a search of someone to whom he could explain. But the editorials had done their work. The doorman at the club presented him with a letter from the House Committee saying that, at a special meeting, it had been decided that he had placed himself in a position offensive to the loyal members of the club and that it was with deep regret that they informed him, etc. As he stumbled out into the street, he heard someone whisper to an out-of-town friend, "There goes Emma Goldman's husband."

As the days went by, things grew unbelievably worse. He was referred to in public meetings whenever an example of civic treachery was in order. A signed advertisement in the newspapers protesting, on behalf of the lineal descendants of the Grand Duke Sergius, against the spread of Bolshevism in northern New Jersey, mentioned a few prominent snakes in the grass, such as Trotzky, Victor Berger, Horace W. Peters, and Emma Goldman.

Then something snapped. Peters began to let his hair grow long and neglected his linen. Each time he was snubbed on the street he uttered a queer guttural sound and made a mark in a little book he carried about with him. He bought a copy of "Colloquial Russian at a Glance," and began picking out inflammatory sentences from the Novy Mir. His wife packed up and went to stay with her sister when he advocated, one night at dinner, the communization of women. The last prop of respectability having been removed, the descent was easy. Emma Goldman, was it? Very well, then, Emma Goldman it should be! Bolshevist, was he? They had said it! "After all, who is to blame for this?" he mumbled to himself. "Capitalism! Militarism! Those Prussians in the Intelligence Department and the Department of Justice! The damnable bourgeoisie who sit back and read their Times and their Tribune and believe what they read there!" He had tried explanations. He had tried argument. There was only one thing left. He found it on page 112 of a little book of Emma Goldman's that he always carried around with him.

You may have read about Peters the other day. He was arrested, wearing a red shirt over his business cutaway and carrying enough TNT to shift the Palisades back into the Hackensack marshes. He was identified by an old letter in his pocket from Henry Cabot Lodge thanking him for a telegram of congratulation Peters had once sent him on the occasion of a certain speech in the Senate.

The next morning the Times said, editorially, that it hoped the authorities now saw that the only way to crush Bolshevism was by the unrelenting use of force.

THOMAS J. WALSH: TEAPOT DOME (1924)

Source: *Forum*, July 1924: "The True History of Teapot Dome."

Our government is operated on the party system. That system has its vices, but one of its cardinal virtues is that the one party, always standing ready to point out the objections to and the weaknesses of candidates, officials, policies, and measures of the other, better men are advanced as candidates, officials are held to a higher degree of efficiency, and a stricter responsibility and policies demanded by the public interest are pursued. So it is no discredit whatever to either me or my colleagues, if it be the fact, as has been so acrimoniously charged, that no sense of public duty, no detestation of crime, no love of country actuated us, that our activities are and have been, as charged, "pure politics."

With both friends and foes, however, there is an acute curiosity to know the sequence of events which ended in the public disgrace of Fall, by what sinuous and devious route the pursuit which led to his exposure was followed, and to learn of the intellectual processes by which that result was achieved. It is a queer trait of human character that finds gratification in the reading of detective stories. This tale reveals some queer manifestations of the operations of the mass mind.

In the spring of 1922 rumors reached parties interested that a lease had been or was about to be made of Naval Reserve No. 3 in the state of Wyoming,—popularly known, from its local designation, as the Teapot Dome. This was one of three great areas known to contain petroleum in great quantity which had been set aside for the use of the Navy—Naval Reserves No. 1 and No. 2 in California by President Taft in 1912, and No. 3 by President Wilson in 1915. The initial steps toward the creation of these reserves—the land being public, that is, owned by the government—were taken by President Roosevelt, who caused to be instituted a study to ascertain the existence and location of eligible areas, as a result of which President Taft in 1909 withdrew the tracts in question from disposition under the public land laws. These areas were thus set apart with a view to keeping in the ground a great reserve of oil available at some time in the future, more or less remote, when an adequate supply for the Navy could not, by reason of the failure or depletion of the world store, or the exigencies possibly of war, be procured or could be procured only at excessive cost; in other words to ensure the Navy in any exigency the fuel necessary to its efficient operation.

From the time of the original withdrawal order, private interests had persistently endeavored to assert or secure some right to exploit these rich reserves, the effort giving rise to a struggle lasting throughout the Wilson administration. Some feeble attempt was made by parties having no claim to any of the territory to secure a lease of all or a portion of the reserves, but in the main the controversy was waged by claimants asserting rights either legal or equitable in portions of the reserves antedating the withdrawal orders, on the one hand, and the Navy Department on the other. In that struggle Secretary Lane was accused of being unduly friendly to the private claimants, Secretary Daniels being too rigidly insistent on keeping the areas intact. President Wilson apparently supported Daniels in the main in the controversy which became acute and Lane retired from the cabinet, it is said, in consequence of the differences which had thus arisen.

The reserves were created, in the first place, in pursuance of the policy of conservation, the advocates of which, a militant body, active in the Ballinger affair, generally supported the attitude of Secretary Daniels and President Wilson.

They too became keen on the report of the impending lease of Teapot Dome. Failing to get any definite or reliable information at the departments, upon diligent inquiry, Senator Kendrick of Wyoming introduced and had passed by the Senate on April 16, 1922, a resolution calling on the secretary of the interior for information as to the existence of the lease which was the subject of the rumors, in response to which a letter was transmitted by the acting secretary of the interior on April 21, disclosing that a lease of the entire Reserve No. 3 was made two weeks before to the Mammoth Oil Company organized by Harry Sinclair, a spectacular oil operator. This was followed by the adoption by the Senate on April 29, 1922, of a resolution introduced by Senator La Follette directing the Committee on Public Lands and Surveys to investigate the entire subject of leases of the naval oil reserves and calling on the secretary of the interior for all documents and full information in relation to the same.

In the month of June following, a cart-load of documents said to have been furnished in compliance with the resolution was dumped in the committee rooms, and a letter from Secretary Fall to the President in justification of the lease of the Teapot Dome and of leases of limited areas on the other reserves was by him sent to the Senate. I was importuned by Senators La Follette and Kendrick to assume charge of the investigation, the chairman of the committee and other majority members being believed to be unsympathetic, and assented the more readily because the Federal Trade Commission had just reported that, owing to conditions prevailing in the oil fields of Wyoming and Montana, the people of my state were paying prices for gasoline in excess of those prevailing anywhere else in the Union.

In the letter of Secretary Fall the course taken was said to have been required by the fact that wells in the adjacent Salt Creek field were draining the oil from the Teapot Dome area. As this theory was disputed, two geologists were employed by the committee to make a study of the ground during the summer of 1923, and the committee, on the incoming of their report, entered, on October 22, 1923, upon the inquiry with which it was charged. I had meanwhile caused to be made a somewhat careful but by no means complete examination of the mass of documents furnished the committee by the Department of the Interior, and went into a laborious study of the exhaustive reports made by the experts, much of it of a highly technical character. I undertook a critical analysis of the lease itself and of the lengthy letter of Secretary Fall to the President, and prepared to interrogate him on the stand concerning features of both, with the purpose of bringing out what I conceived to be fatal vices in the one and misrepresentations and weaknesses in the other.

Incidental to this part of the preparation it was necessary to make a careful study of the acts of Congress of February 25, 1920, and June 4, 1920, of the so-called Overman Act, and the statutes touching contracts by the executive departments generally and by the Navy Department specifically. A somewhat intimate familiarity with the laws in relation to the disposition of the public domain and the procedure before the Department of the Interior in connection therewith lightened the task of preparation.

Concurrently with the prosecution of the work outlined, I addressed letters to all journals which had exhibited any special interest in the subject either at the time or since publicity was given to the execution of the Teapot Dome lease, asking for such information as they might be able to give me or for the sources of the statements of facts made in articles appearing in their columns on the subject.

The reports of the experts gave not a little support to the contention that drainage to an appreciable, if not a very considerable, extent was taking place from the Teapot Dome into the Salt Creek wells, contrary to the view expressed by some, whose opinions were entitled to respect, that owing to the geological conditions such a result could not ensue.

This was unfortunate because from the first it was recognized that there would be some migration of oil across the boundary line of Naval Reserve No. 3 which was purposely made to embrace an area beyond what was believed to be the separate Teapot Dome structure, that the oil in it might be safe.

The Geological Survey had reported that some drainage was taking place and had recommended that the situation be met by drilling a row of line wells along the relatively narrow common boundary. The propriety of leasing the whole 9,000 acres should have been mooted rather than the question of whether any drainage was taking place or was to be apprehended. However, the reports of the experts submitted at the first day's session were decidedly favorable to the leasing so far as they went, and, in the popular mind, if one may so speak, when general indifference to the whole subject was the rule, they went the whole length, it being supposed that the only question involved was geological.

The effect of the reports was heightened by the grossest misrepresentation concerning their import, put out by one of the great news agencies, subsequently asserted by it and probably truly, through the error of a careless reporter. A member of the committee gave out the statement that the inquiry would terminate within a day or two. Apathetically, a few reporters listened in the succeeding sessions to the tedious presentation of extracts from official documents and publications setting out the need of an oil reserve, of the wisdom of maintaining a great supply in the ground, and reciting the story of the efforts of private interests to secure a foothold within the reserves.

Secretary Fall being called to the stand, it was disclosed that hardly had the new administration been installed when the determination was arrived at to transfer the administration of the reserves from the Navy Department, to which it had been confided by Congress because it was believed that department was friendly to their preservation, to the Interior Department, suspected of being disposed to tolerate their exploitation, and an order making the transfer bearing date May 30, 1921, over the signature of President Harding was brought to light. No one now seriously contends that the President had any authority to issue such an order, which, however, at the time of its promulgation, notwithstanding that fact and its evil augury, evoked little attention, though the significance of it was not lost on the watchful leaders of the conservation movement, particularly as Secretary Fall was known from his record in the Senate to be far from friendly to the conservation policy.

No one seemed willing to assume any wrong in or even to criticize the acts of the new administration, buttressed by that 7 million majority and guided by the "best minds." Some little dent in the complacent confidence of the public was made at the time the lease was made through the speeches of Senators Kendrick and La Follette, who called attention to the significant fact that its

execution indicated a departure from the settled policy of the government; that it reversed the result of the struggle that had been carried on throughout the preceding administration; that it was made pursuant to negotiations prosecuted in secret and without competitive biddings. But the listlessness of the public was but little disturbed.

Interest flared fitfully later on when Sinclair declared before a Senate Committee that he expected to make $100 million out of the lease, but it was at a low ebb when the hearings began and the reports of the experts chilled whatever there remained. Nevertheless the reversal of the policy to which general adherence had been given, the secrecy which attended the negotiations, the effort to keep from the public information that the lease had been executed, cast about the transaction a suspicion which my study of the facts had heightened until it had passed to conviction. This was strengthened by the examination of Fall and the disclosures made in connection with his testimony. It might be entertaining did time or space permit to specify these in detail. Misstatements of fact in the letter to the President were not infrequent, but more persuasive with me was the total disregard of the plain provisions of the law, and the utterly untenable arguments made to sustain the action that was taken.

To illustrate: Twice in letters to the President upon inquiry from senators, Fall justified the executive order upon the Overman Act and the acts of February 25 and June 4, 1920. Confronted with the Overman Act, he was compelled to admit that by its plain language it had no application. He could find nothing in either of the other acts to justify his reference to them and then fell back on some vague authority arising from the general scheme of our government. He made a futile effort to find some ground for the provision in the contract authorizing the use of the oil to pay the cost of constructing great storage tanks, pursuant to a program of the Navy, which contemplated the construction of public works without authorization by Congress, involving an expenditure mounting up to $102 million.

He took great credit to himself for sagaciously inserting in the lease that the pipeline to be constructed by Sinclair should be a common carrier, which the Interstate Commerce Law made it without any stipulation to that effect. He reiterated the assertion made in his letter to the President that he considered himself the guardian of important military secrets of the government in connection with the leases which he would, under no circumstances, reveal, plainly intimating that those who were trying to pry into the affair were lacking in loyalty and wanting in that fine sense of duty to country by which he was actuated, recalling, to me at least, that cynical saying of Dr. Johnson that patriotism is the last refuge of a scoundrel. He was voluble to a degree.

There followed other witnesses, mainly attachés of the department, who testified about drainage and kindred matters when the committee suspended on November 2 to resume on November 30,

the case being made as to the legality of the leases, which no one in either house of Congress rose to defend on the resolution to begin suit to annul them, and as to the policy of abandoning the purpose to keep the oil in the ground which has, except for a feeble voice lately raised in the House, had no defender in either body. The public, however, so far as the press indicated, remained apathetic.

In the interim, stories had reached me, rumors rather, about some significant land deal in New Mexico—sometimes it was Fall who purchased for Sinclair, again Sinclair who purchased for Fall. They were vague in character, and diligent inquiry revealed no details. The statement above as to the press is too general. A few newspapers early sensed the importance of the revelations, notably the St. Louis Post-Dispatch, the Omaha World Herald, the Raleigh News and Observer, and the Washington Daily News, a Scripps publication. From the Honorable W. B. Colver, editor of the last named, I learned that the Denver Post, which virulently denounced the lease at the outset and then strangely and suddenly quit, had in the summer of 1922 sent a man to New Mexico to investigate the land deal and that he had made a report which, for some reason, the Post had omitted to publish. Rumors of why the Post had changed its policy fed the suspicion with which I viewed the transaction.

Through Colver and his Denver connections I learned that the reporter was friendly but fearful and that his report, still available, was interesting. I had no funds at my command to bring him to Washington. I had no investigator at my service to interview him or anyone. I went before the Committee and asked for a subpoena to require his attendance. Grudgingly, authority for its issuance was awarded. He came with his report and gave the names and addresses of witnesses in New Mexico who could tell of Fall's sudden rise from financial embarrassment, if not impecuniosity, to comparative affluence. He brought certified copies of the records showing the acquisition by Fall of the Harris ranch, of his delinquencies in the matter of his local taxes extending over a period of ten years, and of his liquidation of them in the summer of 1922, and of the shipment of blooded stock from Sinclair's farm in New Jersey to Fall's ranch in New Mexico.

I then dismissed him and secured subpoenas for the New Mexico witnesses, who told the story of Fall's having paid $91,500 for the ranch mentioned — the initial payment of $10,000 having been made in bills taken from a black tin box — of his subsequent purchase of other lands costing $33,000 more, of the installation of a hydroelectric plant at a cost of from $40,000 to $50,000, and of other expenditures in the aggregate approximating $200,000.

I did not enter into that field of inquiry without misgivings. Seeking advice from a friendly associate on the Committee, I was assured that some plausible story would be told and the effort come to naught. I determined, however,

that the duty of the Committee being to investigate, the witnesses should be called, whatever might be the outcome. The significance of their testimony, synchronizing in its details so strangely with Sinclair's visit in his private car to Fall's ranch in the latter part of 1921, an added circumstance of a suspicious character, could not be overlooked and gave rise to obvious consternation among the friends of Fall on the Committee who were, however, reassured by a message from him to the effect that his son-in-law, who was entirely conversant with his business affairs, would come on to explain all.

By this time there was attracted to the committee room an increasing number of representatives of the press, but though the daily reports of the proceedings were reasonably complete, the editorial force seemed oblivious of what was going on. It was at about that stage of the inquiry that I sought through influential friends to arouse the interest of some of the metropolitan papers, which, for one reason or another, might be expected to aid; for I realized that many might be prompted to help should the issue be agitated who would otherwise remain silent. If they made any effort it was fruitless. Doheny coming upon the stand about that time denounced as an "outrage" the bringing of witnesses from New Mexico to besmirch the character of so upright a public official as Albert B. Fall. More recent denunciatory comment on the investigators does not specify Fall or any other particular individual, for that matter. But at that time I was a muck-raker, vilifying worthy public servants.

Still it was up to Fall to tell where the money came from. His son-in-law did not appear according to promise. Fall did not. A statement made by him to the press gave the assurance that a full explanation would be made. Later it was reported in a vague way that he was ill—now in Chicago, now in New York. Reporters were unable to locate him, for they were now on the job. In fact he came to Chicago, went from there to New York, thence to Atlantic City, and to Washington, where he had an interview with Senators Smoot and Lenroot, members of the Committee, and with Will Hayes, late chairman of the Republican National Committee, to whom he told, as he did in a letter to the Committee on December 27, 1923, that he had borrowed $100,000 with which to purchase the Harris Ranch from Edward B. McLean, owner and editor of the Washington Post, then at Palm Beach, Florida, whither Fall speedily betook himself as McLean's guest.

The same volubility which characterized his testimony was in evidence in his written communication to the Committee. It bore intrinsic evidence of being of doubtful veracity. A month had gone by since the damaging evidence had been heard. An honest man would have hastened to take the stand to refute the inferences to which it naturally gave rise and the doubts that it must inevitably have raised. Had such a man been desperately ill he would have told the story on the stand and not sought refuge from cross-examination by sending a letter from his hotel in the city in which the Committee was sitting. Moreover, the knowing ones smiled incredulously at the idea of Ned McLean's having such a sum of money at hand to loan, though rich in property, or of his loaning it if he had it.

Forthwith that gentleman began to exhibit a feverish anxiety lest he be called as a witness, singularly divining what was coming. He communicated by wire with the Committee; he sent lawyers to represent to it and to me that he was ill, that his wife was ill; that it would be dangerous for him to tempt the rigorous climate of Washington at that season of the year; that he had loaned $100,000 to Fall in November or December 1922; that he knew nothing about the facts otherwise; that he would make a written statement under oath if the Committee desired him to attest to the truth of a statement he would send. He begged not to be called to Washington. I was insistent that he appear; other members of the Committee were disposed to be accommodating, and on a record vote on which I and my supporters were outnumbered, it was agreed to take from him a statement and hold in abeyance until it was received his plea to be excused.

In the discussion Senator Smoot suggested that I go to Palm Beach and take his testimony. That seemed to me impracticable in view of the demands upon my time, but leave was given me to submit interrogatories to be answered in connection with his statement. But on attempting to draft such I became convinced that the effort to get the truth by that method would be unavailing and I signified to the Committee my willingness to go to Palm Beach. The proper authority to take his testimony was given and on the 11th of January he confronted me at "The Breakers."

I made the trip in the expectation that he would say that he had made the loan, intending to interrogate him as to the source from which the money was derived. I proposed to trace it to its source, either to his own private funds, kept in his own private account, or to some account earmarked in a manner that would permit following it to some other origin. I suspected that in some way it came from Sinclair and that I could follow it through various banking transactions to that source. It had not occurred to me that it might have come from Doheny, though it had been disclosed—a fact of which Fall omitted to make any mention when on the stand—that the whole of Naval Reserve No. 1 in California, 32,000 acres in area, estimated to contain 250 million barrels of oil, had been on December 11, 1922, leased to Doheny, who afterward told us that he too expected to make $100 million out of his lease secured from Fall in the same secret manner as had characterized the Sinclair deal.

I was dumbfounded when McLean, evidently appreciating that he would be required to tell the bank upon which he drew to make the loan to Fall, should he adhere to his earlier story, frankly admitted that he never did loan the money to Fall, adding that he gave Fall his checks for that sum, which were returned a few days later and destroyed without being cashed, the recipient asserting that he had arranged to secure the necessary elsewhere.

Now the affair could no longer be kept off the front page. Leading news-gatherers sent representatives to Palm Beach to report the proceedings there; but the country was not fully aroused until on January 21 the Roosevelts went on the stand to relate their lurid story, and the climax was reached when on January 24 Doheny voluntarily appeared to tell that on November 30, 1921, he had loaned $100,000 to Fall without security, moved by old friendship and commiseration for his business misfortunes, negotiations between them then pending eventuating in the contract awarded to Doheny on April 25, following, through which he secured, without competition, a contract giving him a preference right to a lease of a large part of Naval Reserve No. 1, to be followed by the lease of the whole of it, as above recited.

Followed the appearance of Fall, forced by the Committee to come before it, after pleading inability on account of illness, to take refuge under his constitutional immunity, a broken man, the cynosure of the morbidly curious that crowded all approaches to the committee room and packed it to suffocation, vindicating the wisdom of the patriarch who proclaimed centuries ago that the way of the transgressor is hard.

CALVIN COOLIDGE: THE DESTINY OF AMERICA (1923)

Source: *The Price of Freedom: Speeches and Addresses*, New York, 1924, pp. 331–353.

Patriotism is easy to understand in America. It means looking out for yourself by looking out for your country. In no other nation on earth does this principle have such complete application. It comes most naturally from the fundamental doctrine of our land that the people are supreme. Lincoln stated the substance of the whole matter in his famous phrase, "government of the people; by the people, and for the people."

The authority of law here is not something which is imposed upon the people; it is the will of the people themselves. The decision of the court here is not something which is apart from the people; it is the judgment of the people themselves. The right of the ownership of property here is not something withheld from the people; it is the privilege of the people themselves. Their sovereignty is absolute and complete. A definition of the relationship between the institutions of our government and the American people entirely justifies the assertion that: "All things were made by them; and without them was not anything made that was made." It is because the American government is the sole creation and possession of the people that they have always cherished it and defended it, and always will.

There are two fundamental motives which inspire human action. The first and most important, to which all else is subordinate, is that of righteousness. There is that in mankind, stronger than all else, which requires them to do right. When that requirement is satisfied, the next motive is that of gain. These are the moral motive and the material motive. While in some particular instance they might seem to be antagonistic, yet always, when broadly considered or applied to society as a whole, they are in harmony. American institutions meet the test of these two standards. They are founded on righteousness, they are productive of material prosperity. They compel the loyalty and support of the people because such action is right and because it is profitable.

These are the main reasons for the formation of patriotic societies. Desiring to promote the highest welfare of civilization, their chief purpose is to preserve and extend American ideals. No matter what others may do, they are determined to serve themselves and their fellowmen by thinking America, believing America, and living America. That faith they are proud to proclaim to all the world.

It is no wonder that the people are attached to America when we consider what it has done and what it represents. It has been called the last great hope of the world. Its simple story is a romance of surpassing interest. Its accomplishments rise above the realm of fable. To live under the privileges of its citizenship is the highest position of opportunity and achievement ever reached by a people.

If there be a destiny, it is of no avail for us unless we work with it. The ways of Providence will be of no advantage to us unless we proceed in the same direction. If we perceive a destiny in America, if we believe that Providence has been the guide, our own success, our own salvation require that we should act and serve in harmony and obedience.

Throughout all the centuries this land remained unknown to civilization. Just at a time when Christianity was at last firmly established, when there was a general advance in learning, when there was a great spiritual awakening, America began to be revealed to the European world. When this new age began, with its new aspirations and its new needs, its new hopes, and its new desires, the shores of our country rose through the mist, disclosing a new hemisphere in which, untrammeled by Old World conventions, new ideals might establish for mankind a new experience and a new life.

Settlers came here from mixed motives, some for pillage and adventure, some for trade and refuge, but those who have set their imperishable mark upon our institutions came from far higher motives. Generally defined, they were seeking a broader freedom. They were intent upon establishing a Christian commonwealth in accordance with the principle of self-government.

They were an inspired body of men. It has been said that God sifted the nations that He might send choice grain into the wilderness. They had a genius for organized society on the foundation of piety, righteousness, liberty, and obedience to law. They brought with them the accumulated wisdom and experience of the ages wherever it contributed to the civilizing power of these great agencies. But the class and caste, the immaterial formalism of the Old World, they left behind. They let slip their grasp upon conventionalities that they might lay a firmer hold upon realities. ...

The main characteristics of those principles [of government] from which all others are deduced is a government of limited and defined powers, leaving the people supreme. The executive has sole command of the military forces, but he cannot raise a dollar of revenue. The legislature has the sole authority to levy taxes, but it cannot issue a command to a single private soldier. The judiciary interprets and declares the law and the Constitution, but it can neither create nor destroy the right of a single individual. Freedom of action is complete, within moral bounds, under the law which the people themselves have prescribed. The individual is supported in his right to follow his own choice, live his own life, and reap the rewards of his own effort. Justice is administered by impartial courts. It is a maxim of our law that there is no wrong without a remedy. All the power and authority of the whole national government cannot convict the most humble individual of a crime, save on the verdict of an impartial jury composed of twelve of his peers. Opportunity is denied to none, every place is open, and every position yields to the humblest in accordance with ability and application.

The chief repository of power is in the legislature, chosen directly by the people at frequent elections. It is this body, which is particularly responsive to the public will, and yet, as in the Congress, is representative of the whole nation. It does not perform an executive function. It is not, therefore, charged with the necessity of expedition. It is a legislative body and is, therefore, charged with the necessity for deliberation. Sometimes this privilege may be abused, for this great power has been given as the main safeguard of liberty, and wherever power is bestowed it may be used unwisely. But whenever a legislative body ceases to deliberate, then it ceases to act with due consideration.

That fact in itself is conclusive that it has ceased to be independent, has become subservient to a single directing influence or a small group, either without or within itself, and is no longer representative of the people. Such a condition would not be a rule of the people, but a rule of some unconstitutional power. It is my own observation and belief that the American Congress is the most efficient and effective deliberative body, more untrammeled, more independent, more advised, more representative of the will of the people than any body which legislates for any of the great powers. An independent legislature never deprived the people of their liberty.

Such is America, such is the government and civilization which have grown up around the church, the town meeting, and the schoolhouse. It is not perfect, but it surpasses the accomplishments of any other people. Such is the state of society which has been created in this country, which has brought it from the untrodden wilderness of 300 years ago to its present state of development. Who can fail to see in it the hand of destiny? Who can doubt that it has been guided by a Divine Providence? What has it not given to its people in material advantages, educational opportunity, and religious consolation? Our country has not failed, our country has been a success. You are here because you believe in it, because you believe that it is right, and because you know that it has paid. You are determined to defend it, to support it, and, if need be, to fight for it. You know that America is worth fighting for.

But if our republic is to be maintained and improved it will be through the efforts and character of the individual. It will be, first of all, because of the influences which exist in the home, for it is the ideals which prevail in the homelife which make up the strength of the nation. The homely virtues must continue to be cultivated. The real dignity, the real nobility of work must be cherished. It is only through industry that there is any hope for individual development. The viciousness of waste and the value of thrift must continue to be learned and understood. Civilization rests on conservation. To these there must be added religion, education, and obedience to law. These are the foundation of all character in the individual and all hope in the nation. ...

A growing tendency has been observed of late years to think too little of what is really the public interest and too much of what is supposed to be class interest. The two great political parties of the nation have existed for the purpose, each in accordance with its own principles, of undertaking to serve the interests of the whole nation. Their members of the Congress are chosen with that great end in view. Patriotism does not mean a regard for some special section or an attachment for some special interest, and a narrow prejudice against other sections and other interests; it means a love of the whole country. This does not mean that any section or any interest is to be disproportionately preferred or disproportionately disregarded, but that the welfare of all is equally to be sought. Agriculture, transportation, manufacturing, and all the other desirable activities should serve in accordance with their strength and should be served in accordance with the benefits they confer.

A division of the people or their representatives in accordance with any other principle or theory is contrary to the public welfare. An organization for the purpose of serving some special interest is perfectly proper and may be exceedingly helpful, but whenever it undertakes to serve that interest by disregarding the welfare of other interests, it becomes harmful alike to the interest which it proposes to serve and to the public welfare in general. Under the modern organization of society there is such a necessary community of interests that all necessarily experience depression or prosperity together.

They cannot be separated. Our country has resources sufficient to provide in abundance for everybody. But it cannot confer a disproportionate share upon anybody. There is work here to keep amply employed every dollar of capital and every hand of honest toil, but there is no place for profiteering, either in high prices or in low, by the organized greed of money or of men. The most pressing requirement of the present day is that we should learn this lesson and be content with a fair share, whether it be the returns from invested capital or the rewards of toil. On that foundation there is a guarantee of continued prosperity, of stable economic conditions, of harmonious social relationships, and of sound and enduring government. On any other theory or action the only prospect is that of wasteful conflict and suffering in our economic life and factional discord and trifling in our political life. No private enterprise can succeed unless the public welfare be held supreme.

Another necessity of the utmost urgency in this day, a necessity which is worldwide, is economy in government expenditures. This may seem the antithesis of military preparation, but, as a matter of fact, our present great debt is due, in a considerable extent, to creating our last military establishment under the condition of war haste and war prices, which added enormously to its cost. There is no end of the things which the government could do, seemingly, in the way of public welfare, if it had the money. Everything we want cannot be had at once. It must be earned by toilsome labor. There is a very decided limit to the amount which can be raised by taxation without ruinously affecting the people of the country by virtual confiscation of a part of their past savings.

The business of the country, as a whole, is transacted on a small margin of profit. The economic structure is one of great delicacy and sensitiveness. When taxes become too burdensome, either the price of commodities has to be raised to a point at which consumption is so diminished as greatly to curtail production, or so much of the returns from industry is required by the government that production becomes unprofitable and ceases for that reason. In either case there is depression, lack of employment, idleness of investment and of wage earner, with the long line of attendant want and suffering on the part of the people. After order and liberty, economy is one of the highest essentials of a free government. It was in no small degree the unendurable burden of taxation which drove Europe into the Great War. Economy is always a guarantee of peace.

It is the great economic question of government finances which is burdening the people of Europe at the present time. How to meet obligations is the chief problem on continental Europe and in the British Isles. It cannot be doubted that high taxes are the chief cause for the extended condition of unemployment which has required millions to subsist on the public treasury in Great Britain for a long period of time, though the number of these unfortunate people has been declining. A government which requires of the people the contribution of the bulk of their substance and rewards cannot be classed as a free government, or long remain as such. It is gratifying to observe, in our own national government, that there has been an enormous decrease in expenditures, a large reduction of the debt, and a revision of taxation affording great relief.

But it is in peace that there lies the greatest opportunity for relief from burdensome taxation. Our country is at peace, not only legal but actual, with all other peoples. We cherish peace and goodwill toward all the earth, with a sentiment of friendship and a desire for universal well-being. If we want peace it is our business to cultivate goodwill. It was for the promotion of peace that the Washington Conference on the Limitation of Armaments and Pacific Questions was called. For the first time in history the great powers of the earth have agreed to a limitation of naval armaments. This was brought about by American initiative in accordance with an American plan, and executed by American statesmanship. Out of regard for a similar principle is the proposal to participate in the establishment of a World Court. These are in accordance with a desire to adjust differences between nations, not by an overpowering display or use of force but by mutual conference and understanding in harmony with the requirement of justice and of honor.

Our country does not want war, it wants peace. It has not decreed this memorial season as an honor to war, with its terrible waste and attendant train of suffering and hardship which reaches onward into the years of peace. Yet war is not the worst of evils, and these days have been set apart to do honor to all those, now gone, who made the cause of America their supreme choice. Some fell with the word of Patrick Henry, "Give me liberty, or give me death," almost ringing in their ears. Some heard that word across the intervening generations and were still obedient to its call. It is to the spirit of those men, exhibited in all our wars, to the spirit that places the devotion to freedom and truth above the devotion to life, that the nation pays its ever enduring mark of reverence and respect.

It is not that principle that leads to conflict but to tranquillity. It is not that principle which is the cause of war but the only foundation for an enduring peace. There can be no peace with the forces of evil. Peace comes only through the establishment of the supremacy of the forces of good. That way lies only through sacrifice. It was that the people of our country might live in a knowledge of the truth that these, our countrymen, are dead. "Greater love hath no man than this, that a man lay down his life for his friends."

This spirit is not dead, it is the most vital thing in America. It did not flow from any act of government. It is the spirit of the people themselves. It justifies faith in them and faith in their institutions. Remembering all that it has accomplished from the day of the Puritan and Cavalier to the day of the last, least immigrant, who lives by it no less than they, who shall dare to doubt it, who shall dare to challenge it, who shall venture to rouse it into action? Those who have scoffed at it from the day of the Stuarts and the Bourbons to the day of the Hapsburgs and the Hohenzollerns have seen it rise and prevail over them. Calm, peaceful, puissant, it remains, conscious of its authority, "slow to anger, plenteous in mercy," seeking not to injure but to serve, the safeguard of the republic, still the guarantee of a broader freedom, the supreme moral power of the world. It is in that spirit that we place our trust. It is to that spirit again, with this returning year, we solemnly pledge the devotion of all that we have and are.

HARRY EMERSON FOSDICK: THE FUNDAMENTALIST CONTROVERSY (1922)

Source: *The Christian Work*, CII, June 10, 1922, pp. 716–722: "Shall the Fundamentalists Win?"

This morning we are to think of the Fundamentalist controversy which threatens to divide the American churches as though already they were not sufficiently split and riven. A scene, suggestive for our thought, is depicted in the fifth chapter of the Book of the Acts, where the

Jewish leaders hale before them Peter and other of the apostles because they had been preaching Jesus as the Messiah. Moreover, the Jewish leaders propose to slay them, when in opposition Gamaliel speaks: "Refrain from these men, and let them alone; for if this counsel or this work be of men, it will be overthrown; but if it is of God ye will not be able to overthrow them; lest haply ye be found even to be fighting against God." ...

Already all of us must have heard about the people who call themselves the Fundamentalists. Their apparent intention is to drive out of the evangelical churches men and women of liberal opinions. I speak of them the more freely because there are no two denominations more affected by them than the Baptist and the Presbyterian. We should not identify the Fundamentalists with the conservatives. All Fundamentalists are conservatives, but not all conservatives are Fundamentalists. The best conservatives can often give lessons to the liberals in true liberality of spirit, but the Fundamentalist program is essentially illiberal and intolerant.

The Fundamentalists see, and they see truly, that in this last generation there have been strange new movements in Christian thought. A great mass of new knowledge has come into man's possession — new knowledge about the physical universe, its origin, its forces, its laws; new knowledge about human history and in particular about the ways in which the ancient peoples used to think in matters of religion and the methods by which they phrased and explained their spiritual experiences; and new knowledge, also, about other religions and the strangely similar ways in which men's faiths and religious practices have developed everywhere.

Now, there are multitudes of reverent Christians who have been unable to keep this new knowledge in one compartment of their minds and the Christian faith in another. They have been sure that all truth comes from the one God and is His revelation. Not, therefore, from irreverence or caprice or destructive zeal but for the sake of intellectual and spiritual integrity, that they might really love the Lord their God, not only with all their heart and soul and strength but with all their mind, they have been trying to see this new knowledge in terms of the Christian faith and to see the Christian faith in terms of this new knowledge.

Doubtless they have made many mistakes. Doubtless there have been among them reckless radicals gifted with intellectual ingenuity but lacking spiritual depth. Yet the enterprise itself seems to them indispensable to the Christian Church. The new knowledge and the old faith cannot be left antagonistic or even disparate, as though a man on Saturday could use one set of regulative ideas for his life and on Sunday could change gear to another altogether. We must be able to think our modern life clear through in Christian terms, and to do that we also must be able to think our Christian faith clear through in modern terms.

There is nothing new about the situation. It has happened again and again in history, as, for example, when the stationary earth suddenly began to move and the universe that had been centered in this planet was centered in the sun around which the planets whirled. Whenever such a situation has arisen, there has been only one way out — the new knowledge and the old faith had to be blended in a new combination. Now, the people in this generation who are trying to do this are the liberals, and the Fundamentalists are out on a campaign to shut against them the doors of the Christian fellowship. Shall they be allowed to succeed?

It is interesting to note where the Fundamentalists are driving in their stakes to mark out the deadline of doctrine around the church, across which no one is to pass except on terms of agreement. They insist that we must all believe in the historicity of certain special miracles, preeminently the virgin birth of our Lord; that we must believe in a special theory of inspiration — that the original documents of the Scripture, which of course we no longer possess, were inerrantly dictated to men a good deal as a man might dictate to a stenographer; that we must believe in a special theory of the Atonement — that the blood of our Lord, shed in a substitutionary death, placates an alienated Deity and makes possible welcome for the returning sinner; and that we must believe in the second coming of our Lord upon the clouds of heaven to set up a millennium here, as the only way in which God can bring history to

a worthy denouement. Such are some of the stakes which are being driven to mark a deadline of doctrine around the church.

If a man is a genuine liberal, his primary protest is not against holding these opinions, although he may well protest against their being considered the fundamentals of Christianity. This is a free country and anybody has a right to hold these opinions or any others if he is sincerely convinced of them. The question is — Has anybody a right to deny the Christian name to those who differ with him on such points and to shut against them the doors of the Christian fellowship? The Fundamentalists say that this must be done. In this country and on the foreign field they are trying to do it. They have actually endeavored to put on the statute books of a whole state binding laws against teaching modern biology. If they had their way, within the church, they would set up in Protestantism a doctrinal tribunal more rigid than the pope's.

In such an hour, delicate and dangerous, when feelings are bound to run high, I plead this morning the cause of magnanimity and liberality and tolerance of spirit. I would, if I could reach their ears, say to the Fundamentalists about the liberals what Gamaliel said to the Jews, "Refrain from these men and let them alone; for if this counsel or this work be of men, it will be everthrown; but if it is of God ye will not be able to overthrow them; lest haply ye be found even to be fighting against God."

That we may be entirely candid and concrete and may not lose ourselves in any fog of generalities, let us this morning take two or three of these Fundamentalist items and see with reference to them what the situation is in the Christian churches. Too often we preachers have failed to talk frankly enough about the differences of opinion which exist among evangelical Christians, although everybody knows that they are there. Let us face this morning some of the differences of opinion with which somehow we must deal.

We may well begin with the vexed and mooted question of the virgin birth of our Lord. I know people in the Christian churches, ministers, missionaries, laymen, devoted lovers of the Lord and servants of the Gospel, who, alike as they are in their personal devotion to the Master, hold quite different points of view about a matter like the virgin birth. Here, for example, is one point of view: that the virgin birth is to be accepted as historical fact; it actually happened; there was no other way for a personality like the Master to come into this world except by a special biological miracle. That is one point of view, and many are the gracious and beautiful souls who hold it. But side by side with them in the evangelical churches is a group of equally loyal and reverent people who would say that the virgin birth is not to be accepted as an historic fact. ... So far from thinking that they have given up anything vital in the New Testament's attitude toward Jesus, these Christians remember that the two men who contributed most to the Church's thought of the divine meaning of the Christ were Paul and John, who never even distantly allude to the virgin birth.

Here in the Christian churches are these two groups of people and the question which the Fundamentalists raise is this — Shall one of them throw the other out? Has intolerance any contribution to make to this situation? Will it persuade anybody of anything? Is not the Christian Church large enough to hold within her hospitable fellowship people who differ on points like this and agree to differ until the fuller truth be manifested? The Fundamentalists say not. They say the liberals must go. Well, if the Fundamentalists should succeed, then out of the Christian Church would go some of the best Christian life and consecration of this generation — multitudes of men and women, devout and reverent Christians, who need the church and whom the church needs.

Consider another matter on which there is a sincere difference of opinion between evangelical Christians: the inspiration of the Bible. One point of view is that the original documents of the Scripture were inerrantly dictated by God to men. Whether we deal with the story of creation or the list of the dukes of Edom or the narratives of Solomon's reign or the Sermon on the Mount or the thirteenth chapter of First Corinthians, they all came in the same way, and they all came as no other book ever came. They were inerrantly dictated; everything there — scientific opinions, medical theories, historical judgments, as well as spiritual insight — is infallible. That is one idea of the Bible's inspiration. But side by side with those who hold it, lovers of the Book as much as they, are multitudes of people who never think about the Bible so. Indeed, that static and mechanical theory of inspiration seems to them a positive peril to the spiritual life. ...

Here in the Christian Church today are these two groups, and the question which the Fundamentalists have raised is this — Shall one of them drive the other out? Do we think the cause of Jesus Christ will be furthered by that? If He should walk through the ranks of his congregation this morning, can we imagine Him claiming as His own those who hold one idea of inspiration and sending from Him into outer darkness those who hold another? You cannot fit the Lord Christ into that Fundamentalist mold. The church would better judge His judgment. For in the Middle West the Fundamentalists have had their way in some communities and a Christian minister tells us the consequences. He says that the educated people are looking for their religion outside the churches.

Consider another matter upon which there is a serious and sincere difference of opinion between evangelical Christians: the second coming of our Lord. The second coming was the early Christian phrasing of hope. No one in the ancient world had ever thought, as we do, of development, progress, gradual change as God's way of working out His will in human life and institutions. They thought of human history as a series of ages succeeding one another with abrupt

suddenness. The Graeco-Roman world gave the names of metals to the ages — gold, silver, bronze, iron. The Hebrews had their ages, too — the original Paradise in which man began, the cursed world in which man now lives, the blessed Messianic kingdom someday suddenly to appear on the clouds of heaven. It was the Hebrew way of expressing hope for the victory of God and righteousness. When the Christians came they took over that phrasing of expectancy and the New Testament is aglow with it. The preaching of the apostles thrills with the glad announcement, "Christ is coming!"

In the evangelical churches today there are differing views of this matter. One view is that Christ is literally coming, externally, on the clouds of heaven, to set up His kingdom here. I never heard that teaching in my youth at all. It has always had a new resurrection when desperate circumstances came and man's only hope seemed to lie in divine intervention. It is not strange, then, that during these chaotic, catastrophic years there has been a fresh rebirth of this old phrasing of expectancy. "Christ is coming!" seems to many Christians the central message of the Gospel. In the strength of it some of them are doing great service for the world. But, unhappily, many so overemphasize it that they outdo anything the ancient Hebrews or the ancient Christians ever did. They sit still and do nothing and expect the world to grow worse and worse until He comes.

Side by side with these to whom the second coming is a literal expectation, another group exists in the evangelical churches. They, too, say, "Christ is coming!" They say it with all their hearts; but they are not thinking of an external arrival on the clouds. They have assimilated as part of the divine revelation the exhilarating insight which these recent generations have given to us, that development is God's way of working out His will. ...

And these Christians, when they say that Christ is coming, mean that, slowly it may be, but surely, His will and principles will be worked out by God's grace in human life and institutions, until "He shall see of the travail of His soul and shall be satisfied."

These two groups exist in the Christian churches and the question raised by the Fundamentalists is — Shall one of them drive the other out? Will that get us anywhere? Multitudes of young men and women at this season of the year are graduating from our schools of learning, thousands of them Christians who may make us older ones ashamed by the sincerity of their devotion to God's will on earth. They are not thinking in ancient terms that leave ideas of progress out. They cannot think in those terms. There could be no greater tragedy than that the Fundamentalists should shut the door of the Christian fellowship against such.

I do not believe for one moment that the Fundamentalists are going to succeed. Nobody's intolerance can contribute anything to the solution of the situation which we have described. If, then, the Fundamentalists have no solution of the problem, where may we expect to find it? In two concluding comments let us consider our reply to that inquiry.

The first element that is necessary is a spirit of tolerance and Christian liberty. When will the world learn that intolerance solves no problems? This is not a lesson which the Fundamentalists alone need to learn; the liberals also need to learn it. Speaking, as I do, from the viewpoint of liberal opinions, let me say that if some young, fresh mind here this morning is holding new ideas, has fought his way through, it may be by intellectual and spiritual struggle, to novel positions, and is tempted to be intolerant about old opinions, offensively to condescend to those who hold them and to be harsh in judgment on them, he may well remember that people who held those old opinions have given the world some of the noblest character and the most rememberable service that it ever has been blessed with, and that we of the younger generation will prove our case best, not by controversial intolerance, but by producing, with our new opinions, something of the depth and strength, nobility and beauty of character that in other times were associated with other thoughts. It was a wise liberal, the most adventurous man of his day — Paul the Apostle — who said, "Knowledge puffeth up, but love buildeth up."

Nevertheless, it is true that just now the Fundamentalists are giving us one of the worst exhibitions of bitter intolerance that the churches of this country have ever seen. As one watches them and listens to them he remembers the remark of

General Armstrong of Hampton Institute, "Cantankerousness is worse than heterodoxy." There are many opinions in the field of modern controversy concerning which I am not sure whether they are right or wrong, but there is one thing I am sure of: courtesy and kindliness and tolerance and humility and fairness are right. Opinions may be mistaken; love never is.

As I plead thus for an intellectually hospitable, tolerant, liberty-loving church, I am, of course, thinking primarily about this new generation. We have boys and girls growing up in our homes and schools, and because we love them we may well wonder about the church which will be waiting to receive them. Now, the worst kind of church that can possibly be offered to the allegiance of the new generation is an intolerant church. Ministers often bewail the fact that young people turn from religion to science for the regulative ideas of their lives. But this is easily explicable.

Science treats a young man's mind as though it were really important. A scientist says to a young man, "Here is the universe challenging our investigation. Here are the truths which we have seen, so far. Come, study with us! See what we already have seen and then look further to see more, for science is an intellectual adventure for the truth." Can you imagine any man who is worthwhile turning from that call to the church if the church seems to him to say, "Come, and we will feed you opinions from a spoon. No thinking is allowed here except such as brings you to certain specified, predetermined conclusions. These prescribed opinions we will give you in advance of your thinking; now think, but only so as to reach these results."

My friends, nothing in all the world is so much worth thinking of as God, Christ, the Bible, sin and salvation, the divine purposes for humankind, life everlasting. But you cannot challenge the dedicated thinking of this generation to these sublime themes upon any such terms as are laid down by an intolerant church.

The second element which is needed if we are to reach a happy solution of this problem is a clear insight into the main issues of modern Christianity and a sense of penitent shame that the Christian Church should be quarreling over little matters when the world is dying of great needs. If, during the war, when the nations were wrestling upon the very brink of hell and at times all seemed lost, you chanced to hear two men in an altercation about some minor matter of sectarian denominationalism, could you restrain your indignation? You said, "What can you do with folks like this who, in the face of colossal issues, play with the tiddledywinks and peccadillos of religion?" So, now, when from the terrific questions of this generation one is called away by the noise of this Fundamentalist controversy, he thinks it almost unforgivable that men should tithe mint and anise and cummin, and quarrel over them, when the world is perishing for the lack of the weightier matters of the law, justice, and mercy, and faith. ...

The present world situation smells to heaven! And now, in the presence of colossal problems, which must be solved in Christ's name and for Christ's sake, the Fundamentalists propose to drive out from the Christian churches all the consecrated souls who do not agree with their theory of inspiration. What immeasurable folly!

Well, they are not going to do it; certainly not in this vicinity. I do not even know in this congregation whether anybody has been tempted to be a Fundamentalist. Never in this church have I caught one accent of intolerance. God keep us always so and ever increasing areas of the Christian fellowship; intellectually hospitable, open-minded, liberty-loving, fair, tolerant, not with the tolerance of indifference, as though we did not care about the faith, but because always our major emphasis is upon the weightier matters of the law.

REPORT ON CONDITIONS IN THE SOUTH (1938)

Source: Report on Economic Conditions of the South, Prepared for the President by the National Emergency Council, n.p., n.d., Secs. 2, 5, 9, 11.

SOIL

Nature gave the South good soil. With less than a third of the nation's area, the South contains more than a third of the nation's good farming acreage. It has two-thirds of all the land in America receiving a forty-inch annual rainfall or better. It has nearly half of the land on which crops can grow for six months without danger of frost.

This heritage has been sadly exploited. Sixty-one percent of all the nation's land badly damaged by erosion is in the Southern states. An expanse of Southern farmland as large as South Carolina has been gullied and washed away; at least 22 million acres of once fertile soil has been ruined beyond repair. Another area the size of Oklahoma and Alabama combined has been seriously damaged by erosion. In addition, the sterile sand and gravel washed off this land has covered over a fertile valley acreage equal in size to Maryland.

There are a number of reasons for this wastage:

Much of the South's land originally was so fertile that it produced crops for many years no matter how carelessly it was farmed. For generations thousands of Southern farmers plowed their furrows up and down the slopes, so that each furrow served as a ditch to hasten the runoff of siltladen water after every rain. While many farmers have now learned the importance of terracing their land or plowing it on the contours, thousands still follow the destructive practice of the past.

Half of the South's farmers are tenants, many of whom have little interest in preserving soil they do not own.

The South's chief crops are cotton, tobacco, and corn; all of these are inter-tilled crops—the soil is plowed between the rows, so that it is left loose and bare of vegetation.

The topsoil washes away much more swiftly than from land planted to cover crops, such as clover, soybeans, and small grains. Moreover, cotton, tobacco, and corn leave few stalks and leaves to be plowed under in the fall; and as a result the soil constantly loses its humus and its capacity to absorb rainfall.

Even after harvest, Southern land is seldom planted to cover crops which would protect it from the winter rains. This increases erosion tenfold.

Southeastern farms are the smallest in the nation. The operating units average only seventy-one acres, and nearly one-fourth of them are smaller than twenty acres. A farmer with so little land is forced to plant every foot of it in cash crops; he cannot spare an acre for soil-restoring crops or pasture. Under the customary tenancy system, moreover, he has every incentive to plant all his land to crops which will bring in the largest possible immediate cash return. The landlord often encourages him in this destructive practice of cash-cropping.

Training in better agricultural methods, such as planting soil-restoring crops, terracing, contour plowing, and rotation, has been spreading, but such training is still unavailable to most Southern farmers. Annually the South spends considerably more money for fertilizer than for agricultural training through its land-grant colleges, experiment stations, and extension workers.

Forests are one of the best protections against erosion. Their foliage breaks the force of the rain; their roots bind the soil so that it cannot wash away; their fallen leaves form a blanket of vegetable cover which soaks up the water and checks run-off. Yet the South has cut away a large part of its forest, leaving acres of gullied, useless soil. There has been comparatively little effort at systematic reforestation. Overgrazing, too, has resulted in serious erosion throughout the Southwest.

There is a close relationship between this erosion and floods, which recently have been causing a loss to the nation estimated at about $35 million annually. Rainfall runs off uncovered land much more rapidly than it does from land planted to cover crops or forest. Recent studies indicate that a single acre of typical cornland lost approximately 127,000 more gallons of rainfall in a single year than a similar field planted to grass. Another experiment showed that land sodded in grass lost less than 1 percent of a heavy rain through immediate run-off, while nearby land planted to cotton lost 31 percent. In short, unprotected land not only is in danger of destruction; it also adds materially to the destructive power of the swollen streams into which it drains.

These factors—each one reenforcing all the others—are causing an unparalleled wastage of the South's most valuable asset, its soil. They are steadily cutting down its agricultural income and steadily adding to its cost of production as compared with other areas of the world which raise the same crops.

For example, it takes quantities of fertilizer to make worn-out, eroded land produce. The South, with only one-fifth of the nation's income, pays three-fifths of the nation's fertilizer bill. In 1929 it bought 512 million tons of commercial fertilizer at a cost of $161 million. And although fertilizer performs a valuable and necessary service, it does not restore the soil. For a year or two it may nourish a crop, but the land still produces meagerly and at high cost.

Moreover, Southern farmers cannot pile on fertilizer fast enough to put back the essential minerals which are washing out of their land. Each year, about 27,500,000 tons of nitrogen and phosphorus compounds are leached out of Southern soil and sent down the rivers to the sea.

The South is losing more than $300 million worth of fertile topsoil through erosion every year. This is not merely a loss of income — it is a loss of irreplaceable capital.

PRIVATE AND PUBLIC INCOME

The wealth of natural resources in the South—its forests, minerals, and fertile soil—benefit the South only when they can be turned into goods and services which its people need. So far the South has enjoyed relatively little of these benefits simply because it has not had the money or credit to develop and purchase them.

Ever since the war between the states, the South has been the poorest section of the nation. The richest state in the South ranks lower in per capita income than the poorest state outside the region. In 1937 the average income in the South was $314; in the rest of the country it was $604, or nearly twice as much.

Even in "prosperous" 1929, Southern farm people received an average gross income of only $186 a year, as compared with $528 for farmers elsewhere. Out of that $186, Southern farmers had to pay all their operating expenses—tools, fertilizer, seed, taxes, and interest on debt—so that only a fraction of that sum was left for the purchase of food, clothes, and the decencies of life. It is hardly surprising, therefore, that such ordinary items as automobiles, radios, and books are relatively rare in many Southern country areas.

For more than half of the South's farm families—the 53 percent who are tenants without land of their own—incomes are far lower. Many thousands of them are living in poverty comparable to that of the poorest peasants in Europe. A recent study of Southern cotton plantations indicated that the average tenant family received an income of only $73 per person for a year's work. Earnings of sharecroppers ranged from $38 to $87 per person, and an income of $38 annually means only a little more than 10 cents a day.

The South's industrial wages, like its farm income, are the lowest in the United States. In 1937 common labor in twenty important industries got 16 cents an hour less than laborers in other sections received for the same kind of work. Moreover, less than 10 percent of the textile workers are paid more than 52.5 cents an hour, while in the rest of the nation 25 percent rise above this level. A recent survey of the South disclosed that the average annual wage in industry was only $865, while in the remaining states it averaged $1,219.

In income from dividends and interest, the South is at a similar disadvantage. In 1937 the per capita income in the South from dividends and interest was only $17.55, as compared with $68.97 for the rest of the country.

Since the South's people live so close to the poverty line, its many local political subdivisions have had great difficulty in providing the schools and other public services necessary in any civilized community. In 1935 the assessed value of taxable property in the South averaged only $463 per person, while in the nine Northeastern states it amounted to $1,370. In other words, the Northeastern states had three times as much property per person to support their schools and other institutions.

Consequently, the South is not able to bring its schools and many other public services up to national standards, even though it tax the available wealth as heavily as any other section. In 1936 the state and local governments of the south collected only $28.88 per person, while the states and local governments of the nation as a whole collected $51.54 per person.

Although the South has 28 percent of the country's population, its federal income-tax collections in 1934 were less than 12 percent of the national total. These collections averaged only $1.28 per capita throughout the South, ranging from 24 cents in Mississippi to $3.53 in Florida.

So much of the profit from Southern industries goes to outside financiers in the form of dividends and interest that state income taxes would produce a meager yield in comparison with similar levies elsewhere. State taxation does not reach dividends which flow to corporation stockholders and management in other states; and, as a result, these people do not pay their share of the cost of Southern schools and other institutions.

Under these circumstances the South has piled its tax burden on the backs of those least able to pay in the form of sales taxes. (The poll tax keeps the poorer citizens from voting in eight Southern states; thus they have no effective means of protesting against sales taxes.) In every Southern state but one, 59 percent of the revenue is raised by sales taxes. In the Northeast, on the other hand, not a single state gets more than 44 percent of its income from this source, and most of them get far less.

The efforts of Southern communities to increase their revenues and to spread the tax burden more fairly have been impeded by the vigorous opposition of interests outside the region which control much of the South's wealth. Moreover, tax revision efforts have been hampered in some sections by the fear that their industries would move to neighboring communities which would tax them more lightly—or even grant them tax exemption for long periods.

The hope that industries would bring with them better living conditions and consequent higher tax revenues often has been defeated by the competitive tactics of the communities themselves. Many Southern towns have found that industries which are not willing to pay their fair share of the cost of public services likewise are not willing to pay fair wages, and so add little to the community's wealth.

LABOR

The rapidly growing population of the South is faced with the problem of finding work that will provide a decent living. Neither on the farm nor in the factory is there the certainty of a continuing livelihood, and thousands of Southerners shift each year from farm to mill or mine and back again to farm.

The insecurity of work in Southern agriculture, its changes in method and its changes in location make the labor problem of the South not simply an industrial labor problem. Neither the farm population nor the industrial workers can be treated separately, because both groups, as a whole, receive too little income to enable their members to accumulate the property that tends to keep people stable. Industrial labor in the South is to a great extent unskilled and, therefore, subject to the competition of recurring migrations from the farm—people who have lost in the gamble of one-crop share farming. On the other hand, the industrial workers, with low wages and long hours, are constantly tempted to return to the farm for another try.

As industries requiring a large proportion of skilled workers have been slow in developing, the unskilled industrial labor in the South is particularly hampered by the competition of unskilled workers from the farms who accept low wages in preference to destitution at home. Much of the South's increase in industrial activity has been brought about by the removal of cotton-goods manufacturing plants to the Southeast from higher wage areas in New England. This backbone of Southern industry ranks nationally as one of the low-wage manufacturing industries. In the South it pays even lower wages than elsewhere.

According to 1937 figures, the pay for the most skilled work in this industry is about 12 cents an hour less in the South than the pay for the same work elsewhere. The figures for the cotton-goods industry also show the large number of low-wage workers and the small number receiving high wages in the South. More than half of the workers in Southern mills earn under 37.5 cents an hour, although in the rest of the country the industry employs less than 10 percent at such low rates. In the South less than one-tenth of the workers are paid more than 52.5 cents an hour, although one-fourth of the workers in the rest of the nation's cotton-goods industry are paid above this rate.

Similar differentials between the South and other regions are found in lumber, furniture, iron and steel, coal mining, and other industries generally. The influence of the farm population's competition is shown in the unskilled occupations where these wage differentials are widest. The average differential in rates for new labor between the South and the rest of the country in twenty of the country's important industries in 1937 amounted to 16 cents an hour.

In spite of longer working hours, the total annual wages show the same discrepancy. The average yearly pay per person in industry and business in the South in 1935 was $865.41, as compared with $1,219.31 for the rest of the country.

Wage differentials are reflected in lower living standards. Differences in costs of living between the Southern cities and cities in the nation as a whole are not great enough to justify the differentials in wages that exist. In 1935 a study of costs of living showed that a minimum emergency standard required a family income of $75.27 a month as an average for all the cities surveyed. The average of costs in Southern cities showed that $71.94 a month would furnish the minimum emergency standard. This would indicate a difference of less than 5 percent in living costs. Industrial earnings for workers are often 30 to 50 percent below national averages.

Low wages and poverty are in great measure self-perpetuating. Labor organization has made slow and difficult progress among the low-paid workers,

and they have had little collective bargaining power or organized influence on social legislation. Tax resources have been low because of low incomes in the communities, and they have been inadequate to provide for the type of education modern industry requires. Malnutrition has had its influence on the efficiency of workers. Low living standards have forced other members of workers' families to seek employment to make ends meet. These additions to the labor market tend further to depress wages.

Low wages have helped industry little in the South. Not only have they curtailed the purchasing power on which local industry is dependent but they have made possible the occasional survival of inefficient concerns. The standard of wages fixed by such plants and by agriculture has lowered the levels of unskilled and semiskilled workers, even in modern and well-managed establishments. While Southern workers, when well-trained and working under modern conditions, are thoroughly efficient producers, there is not enough such employment to bring the wage levels into line with the skill of the workers.

Unemployment in the South has not resulted simply from the Depression. Both in agriculture and industry, large numbers have for years been living only half employed or a quarter employed or scarcely employed at all. In the problem of unemployment in the South, the relation between agriculture and industry becomes notably clear. Over 30 percent of the persons employed on emergency works programs are farmers and farm laborers, as compared to 15.3 percent for the country as a whole. The insecurity of Southern farmers is reflected in these figures. Seasonal wages in agriculture do not provide incomes sufficient to tide workers over the slack seasons. Part-time industrial work does not provide security the year round. As long as the agricultural worker cannot gain assurance of a continuing existence on the farm, he remains a threat to the job, the wages, and the working conditions of the industrial worker.

OWNERSHIP AND USE OF LAND

The farming South depends on cotton and tobacco for two-thirds of its cash income. More than half of its farmers depend on cotton alone. They are one-crop farmers, subjected year after year to risks which would appall the average businessman. All their eggs are in one basket — a basket which can be upset, and often is, by the weather, the boll weevil, or the cotton market.

The boll weevil can be conquered, and weather hazards tend to cancel themselves out as good seasons follow bad; but the cotton market is a sheer gamble. On this gamble nearly 2 million Southern families stake their year's work and everything they own. Their only chance of making a living is tied up with the fluctuations of the world price of cotton. No other similar area in the world gambles its welfare and the destinies of so many people on a single-crop market year after year.

The gamble is not a good one. Few other crops are subject to such violent and unpredictable price variations as cotton. In 1927, cotton farmers got 20 cents a pound for their crop; in 1929 they got 16 cents; in 1931 they got 6 cents; in 1933 they got 10 cents. Only once during the last decade did the price of cotton change less than 10 percent between pickings. Three times in five years it jumped more than 40 percent — once up and twice down.

Because cotton is the cornerstone of the economy of many parts of the South, the merchants, manufacturers, businessmen, and bankers share the hazards of the farmer. The men who finance cotton farming charge high interest rates because their money is subject to far more than the normal commercial risk. As a result, the mortgage debt of Southern farm owners has been growing steadily for the last twenty years. A checkup on forty-six scattered counties in the South in 1934 showed that one-tenth of the farmland was in the hands of corporations, mostly banks and insurance companies, which had been forced to foreclose their mortgages.

This process has forced more than half of the South's farmers into the status of tenants, tilling land they do not own. Whites and Negroes have suffered alike. Of the 1,831,000 tenant families in the region, about 66 percent are white. Approximately half of the sharecroppers are white, living under economic conditions almost identical with those of Negro sharecroppers.

The pattern of Southern tenancy was set at the end of the war between the states, which left thousands of former slave owners with plenty of land but no capital or labor to work it. Hundreds of thousands of former slaves and impoverished whites were willing to work but had no land. The result was the crop-sharing system, under which the land was worked by men who paid for the privilege with a share of their harvest. It was natural under this system that land-owners should prefer to have virtually all the land put in cotton or other cash crops from which they could easily get their money. Consequently, over wide areas of the South, cash-cropping, one-crop farming, and tenant farming have come to mean practically the same thing. Diversification has been difficult because the landlord and tenant usually have not been able to find a workable method of financing, producing, and sharing the return from such crops as garden truck, pigs, and dairy products.

Tenant families form the most unstable part of our population. More than a third of them move every year, and only a small percentage stay on the same place long enough to carry out a five-year crop rotation. Such frequent moves are primarily the result of the traditional tenure system, under which most renters hold the land by a mere spoken agreement, with no assurance that they will be on the same place next season. Less than 2 percent have written leases, which give them security of tenure for more than one year. Under these circumstances the tenant has no incentive to protect the soil, plant cover crops, or keep buildings in repair. On the contrary, he has every reason to mine the soil for every possible penny of immediate cash return.

The moving habit, moreover, is costly. Most renters merely swap farms every few years without gain to themselves or anybody else. The bare cost of moving has been estimated at about $57 per family, or more than $25 million annually for the tenants of the South. Children are taken out of school in midyear and usually fall behind with their studies. It is almost impossible for a family constantly on the move to take an active part in community affairs; and, as a consequence, churches and other institutions suffer. For example, in one area of North Carolina where the percentage of tenancy is low, there were 257 churches with 21,000 members. In a nearby area of high tenancy — with three and one-half times as many people — there were only 218 churches with 17,000 members.

While it is growing more cotton and tobacco than it can use or sell profitably, the South is failing to raise the things it needs. Southern farmers grow at home less than one-fifth of the things they use; four-fifths of all they eat and wear is purchased.

For example, the region has more than half of the nation's farm people, yet it raises less than one-third of the nation's pigs and cattle. Although it has more than a fourth of America's total population, it produces only one-fifth of the country's eggs, milk, and butter, one-seventh of the hay, one-eighth of the potatoes, and one-twelfth of the oats. Consequently, the South must either obtain these things from other regions and pay handling and freight charges or do without.

Too many Southern families have simply done without, and as a result they have suffered severely from malnutrition and dietary diseases. Many common vegetables are rarities in many Southern farming communities, although both soil and climate are extremely favorable to their growth. Production of foodstuffs could be increased manyfold in the South without infringing on the markets of any other region; most of the increased output could, and should, be absorbed by the very farm families producing it.

Because they have concentrated on cash crops, Southern farmers have planted relatively little of their land in alfalfa, clover, field peas, and soybeans. These and similar legumes add fertility to the soil and at the same time protect fields against washing and gullying. If widely used, they would help the farmer to protect his investment in his land and take a little of the gamble out of his business.

On the other hand, cotton, tobacco, and corn use up the natural richness of the land with great speed. Fields planted to them year after year wear out and wash away much more quickly than fields on which legumes are planted in rotation with cash crops. Yet six acres of Southern cropland out of every ten are planted one season after another in cotton, tobacco, and corn.

FRANKLIN D. ROOSEVELT: PROGRESS OF THE RECOVERY PROGRAM (1933)

Source: *The Public Papers and Addresses of Franklin D. Roosevelt*, Samuel P. Rosenman, compiler, New York, 1938–1950, Vol. II, pp. 295–303.

For many years the two great barriers to a normal prosperity have been low farm prices and the creeping paralysis of unemployment. These factors have cut the purchasing power of the country in half. I promised action. Congress did its part when it passed the Farm and the Industrial Recovery acts. Today we are putting these two acts to work and they will work if people understand their plain objectives.

First, the Farm Act: It is based on the fact that the purchasing power of nearly half our population depends on adequate prices for farm products. We have been producing more of some crops than we consume or can sell in a depressed world market. The cure is not to produce so much. Without our help the farmers cannot get together and cut production, and the Farm Bill gives them a method of bringing their production down to a reasonable level and of obtaining reasonable prices for their crops. I have clearly stated that this method is in a sense experimental, but so far as we have gone we have reason to believe that it will produce good results.

It is obvious that if we can greatly increase the purchasing power of the tens of millions of our people who make a living from farming and the distribution of farm crops, we shall greatly increase the consumption of those goods which are turned out by industry.

That brings me to the final step—bringing back industry along sound lines.

Last autumn, on several occasions, I expressed my faith that we can make possible by democratic self-discipline in industry general increases in wages and shortening of hours sufficient to enable industry to pay its own workers enough to let those workers buy and use the things that their labor produces. This can be done only if we permit and encourage cooperative action in industry, because it is obvious that without united action a few selfish men in each competitive group will pay starvation wages and insist on long hours of work. Others in that group must either follow suit or close up shop. We have seen the result of action of that kind in the continuing descent into the economic hell of the past four years.

There is a clear way to reverse that process: If all employers in each competitive group agree to pay their workers the same wages—reasonable wages—and require the same hours—reasonable hours—then higher wages and shorter hours will hurt no employer. Moreover, such action is better for the employer than unemployment and low wages, because it makes more buyers for his product. That is the simple idea which is the very heart of the Industrial Recovery Act.

On the basis of this simple principle of everybody doing things together, we are starting out on this nationwide attack on unemployment. It will succeed if our people understand it—in the big industries, in the little shops, in the great cities, and in the small villages. There is nothing complicated about it and there is nothing particularly new in the principle. It goes back to the basic idea of society and of the nation itself that people acting in a group can accomplish things which no individual acting alone could even hope to bring about.

Here is an example. In the Cotton Textile Code and in other agreements already signed, child labor has been abolished. That makes me personally happier than any other one thing with which I have been connected since I came to Washington. In the textile industry—an industry which came to me spontaneously and with a splendid cooperation as soon as the Recovery Act was signed—child labor was an old evil. But no employer acting alone was able to wipe it out. If one employer tried it, or if one state tried it, the costs of operation rose so high that it was impossible to compete with the employers or states which had failed to act. The moment the Recovery Act was passed, this monstrous thing which neither opinion nor law could reach through years of effort went out in a flash. As a British editorial put it, we did more under a Code in one day than they in England had been able to do under the common law in eighty-five years of effort. I use this incident, my friends, not to boast of what has already been done but to point the way to you for even greater cooperative efforts this summer and autumn.

We are not going through another winter like the last. I doubt if ever any people so bravely and cheerfully endured a season half so bitter. We cannot ask America to continue to face such needless hardships. It is time for courageous action, and the Recovery Bill gives us the means to conquer unemployment with exactly the same weapon that we have used to strike down child labor.

The proposition is simply this: If all employers will act together to shorten hours and raise wages, we can put people back to work. No employer will suffer, because the relative level of competitive cost will advance by the same amount for all. But if any considerable group should lag or shirk, this great opportunity will pass us by and we shall go into another desperate winter. This must not happen.

We have sent out to all employers an agreement which is the result of weeks of consultation. This agreement checks against the voluntary codes of nearly all the large industries which have already been submitted. This blanket agreement carries the unanimous approval of the three boards which I have appointed to advise in this, boards representing the great leaders in labor, in industry, and in social service. The agreement has already brought a flood of approval from every state and from so wide a cross-section of the common calling of industry that I know it is fair for all. It is

a plan—deliberate, reasonable, and just—intended to put into effect at once the most important of the broad principles which are being established, industry by industry, through codes. Naturally, it takes a good deal of organizing and a great many hearings and many months to get these codes perfected and signed, and we cannot wait for all of them to go through. The blanket agreements, however, which I am sending to every employer will start the wheels turning now, and not six months from now.

There are, of course, men, a few men, who might thwart this great common purpose by seeking selfish advantage. There are adequate penalties in the law, but I am now asking the cooperation that comes from opinion and from conscience. These are the only instruments we shall use in this great summer offensive against unemployment. But we shall use them to the limit to protect the willing from the laggard and to make the plan succeed.

In war, in the gloom of night attack, soldiers wear a bright badge on their shoulders to be sure that comrades do not fire on comrades. On that principle, those who cooperate in this program must know each other at a glance. That is why we have provided a badge of honor for this purpose, a simple design with a legend, "We do our part," and I ask that all those who join with me shall display that badge prominently. It is essential to our purpose.

Already all the great, basic industries have come forward willingly with proposed codes, and in these codes they accept the principles leading to mass reemployment. But, important as is this heartening demonstration, the richest field for results is among the small employers, those whose contribution will be to give new work for from one to ten people. These smaller employers are indeed a vital part of the backbone of the country, and the success of our plan lies largely in their hands.

Already the telegrams and letters are pouring into the White House—messages from employers who ask that their names be placed on this special Roll of Honor. They represent great corporations and companies, and partnerships and individuals. I ask that even before the dates set in the agreements which we have sent out, the employers of the country who have not already done so—the big fellows and the little fellows—shall at once write or telegraph to me personally at the White House, expressing their intentions of going through with the plan. And it is my purpose to keep posted in the post office of every town a Roll of Honor of all those who join with me.

I want to take this occasion to say to the twenty-four governors who are now in conference in San Francisco that nothing thus far has helped in strengthening this great movement more than their resolutions adopted at the very outset of their meeting, giving this plan their instant and unanimous approval, and pledging to support it in their states.

To the men and women whose lives have been darkened by the fact or the fear of unemployment, I am justified in saying a word of encouragement because the codes and the agreements already approved, or about to be passed upon, prove that the plan does raise wages and that it does put people back to work. You can look on every employer who adopts the plan as one who is doing his part, and those employers deserve well of everyone who works for a living. It will be clear to you, as it is to me, that while the shirking employer may undersell his competitor, the saving he thus makes is made at the expense of his country's welfare.

While we are making this great common effort there should be no discord and dispute. This is no time to cavil or to question the standard set by this universal agreement. It is time for patience and understanding and cooperation. The workers of this country have rights under this law which cannot be taken from them, and nobody will be permitted to whittle them away, but, on the other hand, no aggression is now necessary to attain those rights. The whole country will be united to get them for you. The principle that applies to the employers applies to the workers as well, and I ask you workers to cooperate in the same spirit.

When Andrew Jackson, "Old Hickory," died, someone asked, "Will he go to heaven?" and the answer was, "He will if he wants to." If I am asked whether the American people will pull themselves out of this depression, I answer, "They will if they want to." The essence of the plan is a universal limitation of hours of work per week for any individual by common consent and a universal payment of wages above a minimum, also by common consent. I cannot guarantee the success of this nationwide plan, but the people of this country can guarantee its success.

I have no faith in "cure-alls" but I believe that we can greatly influence economic forces. I have no sympathy with the professional economists who insist that things must run their course and that human agencies can have no influence on economic ills. One reason is that I happen to know that professional economists have changed their definition of economic laws every five or ten years for a very long time, but I do have faith, and retain faith, in the strength of the common purpose and in the strength of unified action taken by the American people.

That is why I am describing to you the simple purposes and the solid foundations upon which our program of recovery is built. That is why I am asking the employers of the nation to sign this common covenant with me — to sign it in the name of patriotism and humanity. That is why I am asking the workers to go along with us in a spirit of understanding and of helpfulness.

FRANKLIN D. ROOSEVELT: RELIEF, RECOVERY, AND REFORM (1934)

Source: *The Public Papers and Addresses of Franklin D. Roosevelt*, Samuel P. Rosenman, compiler, New York, 1938–1950, Vol. III, pp. 312–318.

It has been several months since I have talked with you concerning the problems of government. Since January, those of us in whom you have vested responsibility have been engaged in the fulfillment of plans and policies which had been widely discussed in previous months. It seemed to us our duty not only to make the right path clear, but also to tread that path.

As we review the achievements of this session of the Seventy-third Congress, it is made increasingly clear that its task was essentially that of completing and fortifying the work it had begun in March 1933. That was no easy task, but the Congress was equal to it. It has been well said that while there were a few exceptions, this Congress displayed a greater freedom from mere partisanship than any other peacetime Congress since the administration of President Washington himself. The session was distinguished by the extent and variety of legislation enacted and by the intelligence and goodwill of debate upon these measures.

I mention only a few of the major enactments. It provided for the readjustment of the debt burden through the corporate and municipal bankruptcy acts and the Farm Relief Act. It lent a hand to industry by encouraging loans to solvent industries unable to secure adequate help from banking institutions. It strengthened the integrity of finance through the regulation of securities exchanges. It provided a rational method of increasing our volume of foreign trade through reciprocal trading agreements. It strengthened our naval forces to conform with the intentions and permission of existing treaty rights. It made further advances toward peace in industry through the Labor Adjustment Act.

It supplemented our agricultural policy through measures widely demanded by farmers themselves and intended to avert price-destroying surpluses. It strengthened the hand of the federal government in its attempts to suppress gangster crime. It took definite steps toward a national housing program through an act which I signed today designed to encourage private capital in the rebuilding of the homes of the nation. It created a permanent federal body for the just regulation of all forms of communication, including the telephone, the telegraph, and the radio. Finally, and I believe most important, it reorganized, simplified, and made more fair and just our monetary system, setting up standards and policies adequate to meet the necessities of modern economic life, doing justice to both gold and silver as the metal bases behind the currency of the United States.

In the consistent development of our previous efforts toward the saving and safeguarding of our national life, I have continued to recognize three related steps. The first was relief, because the primary concern of any government dominated by the humane ideals of democracy is the simple principle that in a land of vast resources no one should be permitted to starve. Relief was and continues to be our first consideration.

It calls for large expenditures and will continue in modified form to do so for a long time to come. We may as well recognize that fact. It comes from the paralysis that arose as the aftereffect of that unfortunate decade characterized by a mad chase for unearned riches, and an unwillingness of leaders in almost every walk of life to look beyond their own schemes and speculations.

In our administration of relief we follow two principles: first, that direct giving shall, wherever possible, be supplemented by provision for useful and remunerative work; and second, that where families in their existing surroundings will in all human probability never find an opportunity for full self-maintenance, happiness, and enjoyment, we shall try to give them a new chance in new surroundings.

The second step was recovery, and it is sufficient for me to ask each and every one of you to compare the situation in agriculture and in industry today with what it was fifteen months ago.

At the same time we have recognized the necessity of reform and reconstruction—reform because much of our trouble today and in the past few years has been due to a lack of understanding of the elementary principles of justice and fairness by those in whom leadership in business and finance was placed—reconstruction because new conditions in our economic life as well as old but neglected conditions had to be corrected.

Substantial gains well known to all of you have justified our course. I could cite statistics to you as unanswerable measures of our national progress—statistics to show the gain in the average weekly pay envelope of workers in the great majority of industries—statistics to show hundreds of thousands reemployed in private industries, and other hundreds of thousands given new employment through the expansion of direct and indirect government assistance of many kinds; although, of course, there are those exceptions in professional pursuits whose economic improvement, of necessity, will be delayed. I also could cite statistics to show the great rise in the value of farm products—statistics to prove the demand for consumers' goods, ranging all the way from food and clothing to automobiles, and of late to prove the rise in the demand for durable goods—statistics to cover the great increase in bank deposits, and to show the scores of thousands of homes and of farms which have been saved from foreclosure.

But the simplest way for each of you to judge recovery lies in the plain facts of your own individual situation. Are you better off than you were last year? Are your debts less burdensome? Is your bank account more secure? Are your working conditions better? Is your faith in your own individual future more firmly grounded?

Also, let me put to you another simple question: Have you as an individual paid too high a price for these gains? Plausible self-seekers and theoretical diehards will tell you of the loss of individual liberty. Answer this question also out of the facts of your own life. Have you lost any of your rights or liberty or constitutional freedom of action and choice? Turn to the Bill of Rights of the Constitution, which I have solemnly sworn to maintain and under which your freedom rests secure. Read each provision of that Bill of Rights and ask yourself whether you personally have suffered the impairment of a single jot of these great assurances. I have no question in my mind as to what your answer will be. The record is written in the experiences of your own personal lives.

In other words, it is not the overwhelming majority of the farmers or manufacturers or workers who deny the substantial gains of the past year. The most vociferous of the doubting Thomases may be divided roughly into two groups: first, those who seek special political privilege; and second, those who seek special financial privilege. About a year ago I used as an illustration the 90 percent of the cotton manufacturers of the United States who wanted to do the right thing by their employees and by the public but were prevented from doing so by the 10 percent who undercut them by unfair practices and un-American standards. It is well for us to remember that humanity is a long way from being perfect and that a selfish minority in every walk of life—farming, business, finance, and even government service itself—will always continue to think of themselves first and their fellow beings second.

In the working out of a great national program which seeks the primary good of the greater number, it is true that the toes of some people are being stepped on and are going to be stepped on. But these toes belong to the comparative few who seek to retain or to gain position or riches or both by some shortcut which is harmful to the greater good.

In the execution of the powers conferred on it by Congress, the administration needs and will tirelessly seek the best ability that the country affords. Public service offers better rewards in the opportunity for service than ever before in our history — not great salaries but enough to live on. In the building of this service there are coming to us men and women with ability and courage from every part of the Union. The days of the seeking of mere party advantage through the misuse of public power are drawing to a close. We are increasingly demanding and getting devotion to the public service on the part of every member of the administration, high and low.

The program of the past year is definitely in operation and that operation month by month is being made to fit into the web of old and new conditions. This process of evolution is well illustrated by the constant changes in detailed organization and method going on in the National Recovery Administration. With every passing month we are making strides in the orderly handling of the relationship between employees and employers. Conditions differ, of course, in almost every part of the country and in almost every industry. Temporary methods of adjustment are being replaced by more permanent machinery and, I am

glad to say, by a growing recognition on the part of employers and employees of the desirability of maintaining fair relationships all around.

So also, while almost everybody has recognized the tremendous strides in the elimination of child labor, in the payment of not less than fair minimum wages, and in the shortening of hours, we are still feeling our way in solving problems which relate to self-government in industry, especially where such self-government tends to eliminate the fair operation of competition.

In this same process of evolution we are keeping before us the objectives of protecting, on the one hand, industry against chiselers within its own ranks, and, on the other hand, the consumer through the maintenance of reasonable competition for the prevention of the unfair skyrocketing of retail prices.

But, in addition to this our immediate task, we must still look to the larger future. I have pointed out to the Congress that we are seeking to find the way once more to well-known, long-established but to some degree forgotten ideals and values. We seek the security of the men, women, and children of the nation.

That security involves added means of providing better homes for the people of the nation. That is the first principle of our future program. The second is to plan the use of land and water resources of this country to the end that the means of livelihood of our citizens may be more adequate to meet their daily needs. And, finally, the third principle is to use the agencies of government to assist in the establishment of means to provide sound and adequate protection against the vicissitudes of modern life — in other words, social insurance.

Later in the year I hope to talk with you more fully about these plans.

A few timid people who fear progress will try to give you new and strange names for what we are doing. Sometimes they will call it "Fascism," sometimes "Communism," sometimes "Regimentation," sometimes "Socialism." But, in so doing, they are trying to make very complex and theoretical something that is really very simple.

I believe in practical explanations and in practical policies. I believe that what we are doing today is a necessary fulfillment of what Americans have always been doing — a fulfillment of old and tested American ideals.

Let me give you a simple illustration:

While I am away from Washington this summer, a long-needed renovation of and addition to our White House Office Building is to be started. The architects have planned a few new rooms built into the present all-too-small, one-story structure. We are going to include in this addition and in this renovation modern electric wiring and modern plumbing and modern means of keeping the offices cool in the hot Washington summers. But the structural lines of the old Executive Office Building will remain. The artistic lines of the White House buildings were the creation of master builders when our republic was young. The simplicity and the strength of the structure remain in

the face of every modern test. But within this magnificent pattern, the necessities of modern government business require constant reorganization and rebuilding.

If I were to listen to the arguments of some prophets of calamity who are talking these days, I should hesitate to make these alterations. I should fear that while I am away for a few weeks the architects might build some strange new Gothic tower or a factory building or perhaps a replica of the Kremlin or of the Potsdam Palace. But I have no such fears. The architects and builders are men of common sense and of artistic American tastes. They know that the principles of harmony and of necessity itself require that the building of the new structure shall blend with the essential lines of the old. It is this combination of the old and the new that marks orderly peaceful progress, not only in building buildings but in building government itself. Our new structure is a part of and a fulfillment of the old.

All that we do seeks to fulfill the historic traditions of the American people. Other nations may sacrifice democracy for the transitory stimulation of old and discredited autocracies. We are restoring confidence and well-being under the rule of the people themselves. We remain, as John Marshall said a century ago, "emphatically and truly, a government of the people." Our government "in form and in substance ... emanates from them. Its powers are granted by them, and are to be exercised directly on them, and for their benefits."

Before I close, I want to tell you of the interest and pleasure with which I look forward to the trip on which I hope to start in a few days. It is a good thing for everyone who can possibly do so to get away at least once a year for a change of scene. I do not want to get into the position of not being able to see the forest because of the thickness of the trees.

I hope to visit our fellow Americans in Puerto Rico, in the Virgin Islands, in the Canal Zone, and in Hawaii. And, incidentally, it will give me an opportunity to exchange a friendly word of greeting with the presidents of our sister republics, Haiti and Colombia and Panama.

After four weeks on board ship, I plan to land at a port in our Pacific Northwest, and then will come the best part of the whole trip, for I am hoping to inspect a number of our new great national projects on the Columbia, Missouri, and Mississippi rivers, to see some of our national parks and, incidentally, to learn much of actual conditions during the trip across the continent back to Washington.

While I was in France during the War, our boys used to call the United States "God's country." Let us make it and keep it "God's country."

HENRY A. WALLACE: DECLARATION OF INTERDEPENDENCE (1933)

Source: Library of Congress, Wallace Papers.

The new Farm Act signed by President Roosevelt yesterday comprises twenty-six pages of legal document, but the essence of it can be stated simply. It has three main parts. The word "adjustment" covers all three.

First, the administration is empowered to adjust farm production to effective demand as a means of restoring the farmer's purchasing power. The secretary of agriculture is charged to administer this adjustment and to direct, at the same time, an effort to reduce those wastes of distribution which now cause food to pile up, unused, while people go hungry a hundred miles away.

Second is an accompanying authorization to refinance and readjust farm mortgage payments. ...

In the third part of the act, the power for controlled inflation is delegated to the President, and this too signifies adjustment — adjustment of currency and credit to our changed needs. My own responsibility, however, as secretary of agriculture is solely with the first part of the act.

It should be made plain at the outset that the new Farm Act initiates a program for a general advance in buying power, and advance that must extend throughout America, lightening the way of the people in city and country alike. We must lift urban buying power as we lift farm prices. The Farm Act must not be considered an isolated advance in a restricted sector; it is an important part of a large-scale, coordinated attack on the whole problem of depression.

If enough people will join in the wide and swift adjustments that this act proposes, we can make it work. I say if because this act is not a hand-out measure. It does provide new governmental machinery which can be used by all who labor to grow and to bring us food and fabrics, to organize, to put their businesses in order, and to make their way together out of a wilderness of economic desolation and waste.

But the machinery will not work itself. The farmers and the distributors of food-stuffs must use it and make it work. The government can help map lines of march and can see that the interest of no one group is advanced out of line with the interest of all. But government officials cannot and will not go out and work for private businesses. A farm is a private business; so is a farmers' cooperative; and so are all the great links in the food-distributing chain. Government men cannot and will not go out and plow down old trails for agriculture or build for the distributing industries new roads out of the woods. The growers, the processors, the carriers and sellers of food must do that for themselves.

Following trade agreements, openly and democratically arrived at, with the consumer at all times represented and protected from gouging, these industries must work out their own salvation. They must put an end to cutthroat competition and wasteful disorder. The Emergency Adjustment Act makes it lawful and practical for them to get together and do so. It provides for a control of production to accord with actual need and for an orderly distribution of essential supplies.

In the end, we envision programs of planned land use, and we must turn our thought to this end immediately; for many thousands of refugees from urban pinch and hunger are turning, with little or no guidance, to the land. A tragic number of city families are reoccupying abandoned farms, farms on which born farmers, skilled, patient, and accustomed to doing with very little, were unable to make a go of it. In consequence of this backflow there are now 32 million people on the farms of the United States, the greatest number ever recorded in our history. Some of those who have returned to farming will find their place there, but most of them, I fear, will not.

I look to a day when men and women will be able to do in the country the work that they have been accustomed to do in the city; a day when we shall have more industrial workers out in the open where there is room to live. I look to a decentralization of industry; and hope that out of this Adjustment Act will come, in time, a resettlement of America. But in this respect we shall have to make haste slowly. We do not need any more farmers out in the country now. We do need more people there with some other means of livelihood, buying, close at hand, farm products; enriching and making more various the life of our open-country and village communities.

In adjusting our production of basic foods and fabrics, our first need is to plant and send to market less wheat, less cotton, less corn, fewer hogs, and less of other basic crops whereof already we have towering surpluses, with no immediate prospect of clearance beyond the sea. The act authorizes the secretary of agriculture to apply excise taxes on the processing of these products and to pay the money thus derived to farmers who agree to enter upon programs of planned production, and who abide by that agreement. There are increasing possibilities that by trade agreements we may be able on certain crops or livestock products to arrive at a balanced abundance without levying a tax on the product at any point. In no case will taxes be levied on products purchased for the unemployed.

What it amounts to is an advance toward higher prices all along the line. Current proposals for government cooperation with industry are really at one with this Farm Act. Unless we can get reemployment going, lengthen payrolls, and shorten breadlines, no effort to lift prices can last very long. Our first effort as to agriculture will be to seek markets and to adjust production downward, with safe margins to provide enough food for all. This effort we will continue until such time as diminishing stocks raise prices to a point where the farmer's buying power will be as high as it was in the prewar years, 1909 to 1914.

The reason that we chose that period is because the prices farmers got for their crops in those years and the prices they paid for manufactured goods and urban services most nearly approached an equitable relationship. There was thus a balance between our major producing groups. At that time there was not the terrific disparity between rural and urban purchasing power which now exists and which is choking the life out of all forms of American business.

We do not propose to reduce agricultural production schedules to a strictly domestic basis. Our foreign trade has dwindled to a mere trickle; but we still have some foreign customers for farm products; we want to keep that trade, if possible, and to get more foreign trade, if we can. The immediate job, as I see it now, is to organize American agriculture to reduce its output to domestic need, plus that amount which we can export at a profit.

If, within a year or so, it happens that the world tide turns and world trade revives, we still can utilize to excellent advantage our crop adjustment and controlled distribution setup. We can find out how much they really want over there, and at what price; and then we can take off the brakes and step on the gas a little at a time, deliberately, not recklessly and blindly, as we have in times past. We can speed up just enough to meet that demand for our products which will return a decent price.

The first sharp downward adjustment is necessary because during the past years we have defiantly refused to face an overwhelming reality. In consequence, changed world conditions bear down on us so heavily as to threaten our national life. In the years immediately before the war, our agriculture was tending toward a domestic basis of production. The war rushed us out upon the markets of the world. Fifty million acres of Europe, not counting Russia, went out of cultivation. Food prices rose. A new surge of pioneers strode forth upon those high and dusty plains once called the Great American Desert and found that they could grow wheat there. Throughout the country, sod was broken. America entered the war. American farmers stepped out to serve the nation as American boys stepped up in answer to the call. Before the surge was over, we had put to the plow a vast new area. To replace the 50 million lost acres of Europe, America had added 30 million acres to its tilled domain and thrown its whole farm plant into high gear. ...

The oversupplied situation began as a result of the war. As early as 1920 American agriculture was served notice that martial adventures must be paid for afterward, through the nose. The agricultural deflation was well under way by 1923; half of Montana's wheat farmers had by that time lost their farms. In 1929, the agricultural deflation became a plunge. Today, agriculture is twice as much deflated as general industry; and its prices are down 40 percent below the level of prices in general.

Ever since 1920, hundreds of thousands of farm families have had to do without civilized goods and services which in normal times they were glad and eager to buy. Since 1929, millions of farm people have had to patch their garments, store their cars and tractors, deprive their children of educational opportunities, and cease, as farmers, to improve their practices and their property. They have been forced to let their homes and other buildings stand bare and unpainted, eaten by time and the weather. They have been driven toward peasant, or less than peasant, standards; they have been forced to adopt frontier methods of bare sustenance at a time when in the old surging, unlimited sense of the word we have no longer a frontier.

When the farmer gets higher prices, he will start spending. He will have to. He needs things. He needs new shoes and clothing for all the family so that his children can go to school in any weather with dry feet, protected bodies, and a decent American feeling of equality and pride. ...

To reorganize agriculture, cooperatively, democratically, so that the surplus lands on which men and women now are toiling, wasting their time, wearing out their lives to no good end shall be taken out of production — that is a tremendous task. The adjustment we seek calls, first of all, for a mental adjustment, a willing reversal of driving, pioneer opportunism and ungoverned laissez-faire. The ungoverned push of rugged individualism perhaps had an economic justification in the days when we had all the West to surge upon and conquer; but this country has filled up now and grown up. There are no more Indians to fight. No more land worth taking may be had for the grabbing. We must experience a change of mind and heart.

The frontiers that challenge us now are of the mind and spirit. We must blaze new trails in scientific accomplishment, in the peaceful arts and industries. Above all, we must blaze new trails in the direction of a controlled economy, common sense, and social decency. ...

This Farm Act differs from the partway attacks on the problems that have been launched in the past. This act provides for controlled production. Without that, no price-lifting effort can possibly work; because if there is no control of acreage, the better price increases the next year's planting and the greater harvest wrecks the price.

For example, I would call to your attention that Chicago wheat is 13 cents above Liverpool, whereas ordinarily it is 15 cents below. We are 28 cents out of line with our customary export situation because the new wheat crop is 250 million bushels below normal. It is obvious, therefore, that with ordinary weather conditions next winter and spring we can easily have a crop which will result in prices again being 15 cents below Liverpool in this country. I am saying this because I do not want the wheat farmers of this country to live too long in a fool's paradise. ...

Our immediate job is to decide what products to concentrate on, what methods of production adjustment to employ on them, to determine to what extent marketing agreements can be useful, and to appraise the necessity for and rates of processing taxes.

To help us in these determinations, as rapidly as possible, we shall have here in Washington representatives of agriculture and representatives of the processing and distributing trades. These men and women will take part in commodity conferences, and in the light of their technical knowledge will suggest which of the several plans of attack will work best for different crops and regions. Bearing their recommendations in mind, we shall decide just what action to take and when to take it. As each decision is made, we shall get it out directly and publicly to the farmers affected and launch organization efforts throughout the nation.

As President Roosevelt indicated at Topeka last September, the right sort of farm and national relief should encourage and strengthen farmer cooperation. I believe we have in this new law the right sort of stimulus to that end.

I want to say, finally, that unless, as we lift farm prices, we also unite to control production, this plan will not work for long. And the only way we can effectively control production for the long pull is for you farmers to organize, and stick, and do it yourselves. This act offers you promise of a balanced abundance, a shared prosperity, and a richer life. It will work if you will make it yours, and make it work.

I hope that you will come to feel in time, as I do now, that the rampageous individualist who signs up for adjustment and then tries to cheat is cheating not only the government but his neighbors. I hope that you will come to see in this act, as I do now, a Declaration of Interdependence; a recognition of our essential unity and of our absolute reliance one upon another.

HUEY P. LONG: SHARING OUR WEALTH (1935)

Source: Congressional Record, Washington, 74 Cong., 1 Sess., pp. 410–412.

President Roosevelt was elected on November 8, 1932. People look upon an elected President as the President. This is January 1935. We are in our third year of the Roosevelt depression, with the conditions growing worse. ...

We must now become awakened! We must know the truth and speak the truth. There is no use to wait three more years. It is not Roosevelt or ruin; it is Roosevelt's ruin.

Now, my friends, it makes no difference who is President or who is senator. America is for 125 million people and the unborn to come. We ran Mr. Roosevelt for the presidency of the United States because he promised to us by word of mouth and in writing:

- That the size of the big man's fortune would be reduced so as to give the masses at the bottom enough to wipe out all poverty; and
- That the hours of labor would be so reduced that all would share in the work to be done and in consuming the abundance mankind produced.

Hundreds of words were used by Mr. Roosevelt to make these promises to the people, but they were made over and over again. He reiterated these pledges even after he took his oath as President. Summed up, what these promises meant was: "Share our wealth."

When I saw him spending all his time of ease and recreation with the business partners of Mr. John D. Rockefeller, Jr., with such men as the Astors, etc., maybe I ought to have had better sense than to have believed he would ever break down their big fortunes to give enough to the masses to end poverty—maybe some will think me weak for ever believing it all, but millions of other people were fooled the same as myself. I was like a drowning man grabbing at a straw, I guess. The face and eyes, the hungry forms of mothers and children, the aching hearts of students denied education were before our eyes, and when Roosevelt promised, we jumped for that ray of hope.

So therefore I call upon the men and women of America to immediately join in our work and movement to share our wealth.

There are thousands of share-our-wealth societies organized in the United States now. We want 100,000 such societies formed for every nook and corner of this country—societies that will meet, talk, and work, all for the purpose that the great wealth and abundance of this great land that belongs to us may be shared and enjoyed by all of us.

We have nothing more for which we should ask the Lord. He has allowed this land to have too much of everything that humanity needs.

So in this land of God's abundance we propose laws, viz.:

- The fortunes of the multimillionaires and billionaires shall be reduced so that no one person shall own more than a few million dollars to the person. We would do this by a capital levy tax. On the first million that a man was worth, we would not impose any tax. We would say, "All right for your first million dollars, but after you get that rich you will have to start helping the balance of us." So we would not levy any capital levy tax on the first million one owned. But on the second million a man owns, we would tax that 1 percent, so that every year the man owned the second million dollars he would be taxed $10,000. On the third million we would impose a tax of 2 percent. On the fourth million we would impose a tax of 4 percent. On the fifth million we would impose a tax of 8 percent. On the sixth million we would impose a tax of 16 percent. On the seventh million we would impose a tax of 32 percent. On the eighth million we would impose a tax of 64 percent; and on all over the eighth million we would impose a tax of 100 percent.

What this would mean is that the annual tax would bring the biggest fortune down to $3 or $4 million to the person because no one could pay taxes very long in the higher brackets. But $3 to $4 million is enough for any one person and his children and his children's children. We cannot allow one to have more than that because it would not leave enough for the balance to have something.

- We propose to limit the amount any one man can earn in one year or inherit to $1 million to the person.
- Now, by limiting the size of the fortunes and incomes of the big men, we will throw into the government Treasury the money and property from which we will care for the millions of people who have nothing; and with this money we will provide a home and the comforts of home, with such common conveniences as radio and automobile, for every family in America, free of debt.
- We guarantee food and clothing and employment for everyone who should work by shortening the hours of labor to thirty hours per week, maybe less, and to eleven months per year, maybe less. We would have the hours shortened just so much as would give work to everybody to produce enough for everybody; and if we were to get them down to where they were too short, then we would lengthen them again. As long as all the people working can produce enough of automobiles, radios, homes, schools, and theaters for everyone to have that kind of comfort and convenience, then let us all have

work to do and have that much of heaven on earth.

- We would provide education at the expense of the states and the United States for every child, not only through grammar school and high school but through to a college and vocational education. We would simply extend the Louisiana plan to apply to colleges and all people. Yes; we would have to build thousands of more colleges and employ 100,000 more teachers; but we have materials, men, and women who are ready and available for the work. Why have the right to a college education depend upon whether the father or mother is so well-to-do as to send a boy or girl to college? We would give every child the right to education and a living at birth.
- We would give a pension to all persons above sixty years of age in an amount sufficient to support them in comfortable circumstances, excepting those who earn $1,000 per year or who are worth $10,000.
- Until we could straighten things out — and we can straighten things out in two months under our program — we would grant a moratorium on all debts which people owe that they cannot pay.

And now you have our program, none too big, none too little, but every man a king.

We owe debts in America today, public and private, amounting to $252 billion. That means that every child is born with a $2,000 debt tied around his neck to hold him down before he gets started. Then, on top of that, the wealth is locked in a vise owned by a few people. We propose that children shall be born in a land of opportunity, guaranteed a home, food, clothes, and the other things that make for living, including the right to education.

Our plan would injure no one. It would not stop us from having millionaires — it would increase them tenfold, because so many more people could make $1 million if they had the chance our plan gives them. Our plan would not break up big concerns. The only difference would be that maybe 10,000 people would own a concern instead of 10 people owning it.

But, my friends, unless we do share our wealth, unless we limit the size of the big man so as to give something to the little man, we can never have a happy or free people. God said so! He ordered it.

We have everything our people need. Too much of food, clothes, and houses — why not let all have their fill and lie down in the ease and comfort God has given us? Why not? Because a few own everything — the masses own nothing.

I wonder if any of you people who are listening to me were ever at a barbecue! We used to go there — sometimes 1,000 people or more. If there were 1,000 people, we would put enough meat and bread and everything else on the table for 1,000 people. Then everybody would be called and everyone would eat all they wanted.

But suppose at one of these barbecues for 1,000 people that one man took 90 percent of the food and ran off with it and ate until he got sick and let the balance rot. Then 999 people would have only enough for 100 to eat and there would be many to starve because of the greed of just one person for something he couldn't eat himself.

Well, ladies and gentlemen, America, all the people of America, have been invited to a barbecue. God invited us all to come and eat and drink all we wanted. He smiled on our land and we grew crops of plenty to eat and wear. He showed us in the earth the iron and other things to make everything we wanted. He unfolded to us the secrets of science so that our work might be easy. God called: "Come to my feast."

Then what happened? Rockefeller, Morgan, and their crowd stepped up and took enough for 120 million people and left only enough for 5 million for all the other 125 million to eat. And so many millions must go hungry and without these good things God gave us unless we call on them to put some of it back.

FRANKLIN D. ROOSEVELT: A PROGRAM FOR SOCIAL SECURITY (1935)

Source: Congressional Record, Washington, 74 Cong., 1 Sess., pp. 545–546.

In addressing you on June 8, 1934, I summarized the main objectives of our American program. Among these was, and is, the security of the men, women, and children of the nation against certain hazards and vicissitudes of life. This purpose is an essential part of our task. In my annual message to you I promised to submit a definite program of action. This I do in the form of a report to me by a Committee on Economic Security, appointed by me for the purpose of surveying the field and of recommending the basis of legislation.

I am gratified with the work of this committee and of those who have helped it: The Technical Board of Economic Security, drawn from various departments of the government; the Advisory Council on Economic Security, consisting of informed and public-spirited private citizens; and a number of other advisory groups, including a Committee on Actuarial Consultants, a Medical Advisory Board, a Dental Advisory Committee, a Hospital Advisory Committee, a Public Health Advisory Committee, a Child Welfare Committee, and an Advisory Committee on Employment Relief. All of those who participated in this notable task of planning this major legislative proposal are ready and willing at any time to consult with and assist in any way the appropriate congressional committees and members with respect to detailed aspects.

It is my best judgment that this legislation should be brought forward with a minimum of delay. Federal action is necessary to and conditioned upon the actions of states. Forty-four legislatures are meeting or will meet soon. In order that the necessary state action may be taken promptly, it is important that the federal government proceed speedily.

The detailed report of the committee sets forth a series of proposals that will appeal to the sound sense of the American people. It has not attempted the impossible nor has it failed to exercise sound caution and consideration of all of the factors concerned: the national credit, the rights and responsibilities of states, the capacity of industry to assume financial responsibilities, and the fundamental necessity of proceeding in a manner that will merit the enthusiastic support of citizens of all sorts.

It is overwhelmingly important to avoid any danger of permanently discrediting the sound and necessary policy of federal legislation for economic security by attempting to apply it on too ambitious a scale before actual experience has provided guidance for the permanently safe direction of such efforts. The place of such a fundamental in our future civilization is too precious to be jeopardized now by extravagant action. It is a sound idea — a sound ideal. Most of the other advanced countries of the world have already adopted it, and their experience affords the knowledge that social insurance can be made a sound and workable project.

Three principles should be observed in legislation on this subject. In the first place, the system adopted, except for the money necessary to initiate it, should be self-sustaining in the sense that funds for the payment of insurance benefits should not come from the proceeds of general taxation. Second, excepting in old-age insurance, actual management should be left to the states, subject to standards established by the federal government. Third, sound financial management of the funds and the reserves and protection of the credit structure of the nation should be assured by retaining federal control over all funds through trustees in the Treasury of the United States.

At this time, I recommend the following types of legislation looking to economic security:

First, unemployment compensation.

Second, old-age benefits, including compulsory and voluntary annuities.

Third, federal aid to dependent children through grants to states for the support of existing mother's pension systems and for services for the protection and care of homeless, neglected, dependent, and crippled children.

Fourth, additional federal aid to state and local public-health agencies and the strengthening of the federal Public Health Service. I am not at this time recommending the adoption of so-called health insurance, although groups representing the medical profession are cooperating with the federal government in the further study of the subject, and definite progress is being made.

With respect to unemployment compensation, I have concluded that the most practical proposal is the levy of a uniform federal payroll tax, 90 percent of which should be allowed as an offset to employers contributing under a compulsory state unemployment compensation act. The purpose of this is to afford a requirement of a reasonably uniform character for all states cooperating with the federal government and to promote and encourage the passage of unemployment compensation laws in the states. The 10 percent not thus offset should be used to cover the costs of federal and state administration of this broad system. Thus, states will largely administer unemployment compensation, assisted and guided by the federal government.

An unemployment compensation system should be constructed in such a way as to afford every practicable aid and incentive toward the larger purpose of employment stabilization. This can be helped by the intelligent planning of both public and private employment. It also can be helped by correlating the system with public employment so that a person who has exhausted his benefits may be eligible for some form of public work as is recommended in this report. Moreover, in order to encourage the stabilization of private employment, federal legislation should not foreclose the states from establishing means for inducing industries to afford an even greater stabilization of employment.

In the important field of security for our old people, it seems necessary to adopt three principles — first, noncontributory old-age pensions for those who are now too old to build up their own insurance; it is, of course, clear that for perhaps thirty years to come funds will have to be provided by the states and the federal government to meet these pensions. Second,

compulsory contributory annuities, which in time will establish a self-supporting system for those now young and for future generations. Third, voluntary contributory annuities by which individual initiative can increase the annual amounts received in old age. It is proposed that the federal government assume one-half of the cost of the old-age pension plan, which ought ultimately to be supplanted by self-supporting annuity plans.

The amount necessary at this time for the initiation of unemployment compensation, old-age security, children's aid, and the promotion of public health, as outlined in the report of the Committee on Economic Security, is approximately $100 million.

The establishment of sound means toward a greater future economic security of the American people is dictated by a prudent consideration of the hazards involved in our national life. No one can guarantee this country against the dangers of future depressions, but we can reduce these dangers. We can eliminate many of the factors that cause economic depressions and we can provide the means of mitigating their results. This plan for economic security is at once a measure of prevention and a method of alleviation.

We pay now for the dreadful consequence of economic insecurity — and dearly. This plan presents a more equitable and infinitely less expensive means of meeting these costs. We cannot afford to neglect the plain duty before us. I strongly recommend action to attain the objectives sought in this report.

JOHN L. LEWIS: INDUSTRIAL UNIONS (1938)

Source: Proceedings of the First Constitutional Convention of the Congress of Industrial Organizations, n.p., n.d., pp. 9–12.

I profoundly appreciate the opportunity of opening this convention with greetings through President Fagan of organized labor in this great industrial section, with the greetings of His Honor, the mayor of Pittsburgh, extended in behalf of the people of this great municipality, with the greetings of the Christian churches, represented by the eminent clergymen who are present this morning, and the acclaim of our own people.

Why these greetings? Why this interest? Why this enthusiasm? Why this acclaim? Because there has been born in America a new, modern labor movement dedicated to the proposition that all who labor are entitled to equality of opportunity, the right to organize, the right to participate in the bounties and the blessings of this country and our government, the right to aspire to an equality of position, and the right to express views, objectives, and rights on a parity with any other citizen, whatever may be his place, his condition of servitude, or the degree of world's goods which he may possess.

So that is the greeting of the Committee for Industrial Organization, assembled here and about to formalize its own internal affairs and make permanent its form of organization.

It is perhaps an interesting coincidence that fifty-seven years ago, almost to the day, the great [Samuel] Gompers founded in this city the labor movement of his generation. That labor movement served that generation in a period where the skills in American trade and industry were the skills of handicraft and not the skills of the machine age and of mass production. But time moves on and the old order changes, and, as the changes became obvious, it was more and more apparent that the labor movement and the type of organization founded in Pittsburgh fifty-seven years ago was not equal to the task of organizing or rendering service to the teeming millions who labor in American industries in this generation of our life.

Perhaps it will be illustrative to say that in fifty-four years of existence and advocation and administration of its affairs, the American Federation of Labor failed to bring to the hundreds of thousands of workers in the industries in the Pittsburgh area the blessings of collective bargaining; and during all those years the Pittsburgh industrial district was the citadel of nonunionism in America, the citadel of labor exploitation, and the recognized fortress of those financial interests and industrial interests in America who preferred to exploit and debase and degrade labor rather than recognize its existence or concede its right to fair treatment.

The old order changes, and what the American Federation of Labor could not do in fifty-four years of agitation the

Committee for Industrial Organization has done in less than three years. Does that mean anything? Ask the workers in these great steel and other industrial plants within 100 miles of downtown Pittsburgh. They will tell you whether or not it means anything, and they will answer the question why they joined the CIO; they will tell you that they were not receiving the aid and succor from the American labor movement which they should have received.

The Pittsburgh area today is the most completely organized city of any city or any area in industrial America. Whether you come into Pittsburgh through the Ohio Valley, the Monongahela Valley, or the gateway of the Allegheny, you pass along miles of great industrial plants; and when you pass one of those great industrial plants in coming through any of those gateways, you pass a plant where the CIO has established collective bargaining and where the employees there are members of the CIO.

To you, Philip Murray, vice-president of the United Mine Workers of America, chairman of the Steel Workers Organizing Committee, my compliments, sir, for this superhuman task that you have accomplished in the area where you live, where the headquarters of your great organization exist. You have rendered a service, not alone to the people of Pittsburgh but to the workers in these great industries; you have rendered an outstanding and superb service to the labor movement of America, to our country, and to our flag.

In the light of that record which I have merely portrayed as indicating the events that have transpired in this area, and which may be duplicated ad infinitum in other areas, in the light of that record, why should the CIO as a movement be criticized, opposed, slandered, and vilified, denounced from the street corners by its adversaries, and constantly opposed in high places when it offers to the community, to the state, and to the nation a program of rational procedure and orderly conduct, a program of working out in a peaceful way the problems that encumber the relations of labor and industry and finance in this country?

In this steel industry to which I may aptly refer because of our presence here today, Mr. Murray and the Steel Workers organization have contracts with more than 540 corporate entities engaged in the manufacture and the fabrication of steel; and in every one of those plants, in every one of those corporations without exception, since the negotiation of those agreements, peaceful relations have obtained and mutual satisfaction prevails between management and labor — something of a record of an industry that for a lifetime, through oppressive measures, prevented the organization of its employees and denied to them the right to join the union of their choice.

But why should there be opposition and criticism of a movement that stands for orderly procedure and for a rational working out of the problems of modern industrial relationships; of an organization that is dedicated to the proposition of maintaining and supporting our democratic form of government; of an organization that is dedicated to the proposition of the right of investors to have a profit on their investment; and an organization that maintains the right to the freedom of contract relations between citizens of our republic, that is willing to lend its strength and its resources and its young men at any time to support and maintain that form of government, asking only in return that the safeguards of the Constitution and the Bill of Rights be extended to cover the most lowly, humble worker, as a right, as a privilege for an American?

These are troublous times in the world of affairs. Great and sinister forces are moving throughout the world, and he is optimistic indeed who believes that those forces will not affect Americans and will not have their impact and repercussions upon the peoples of the Western Hemisphere. Democracy is on trial in the world and in the United States. We want to preserve democracy. We cannot preserve democracy here in our own country if we encourage as a people the overwhelming tidal wave of criticism, slander, and abuse for an American institution like the CIO, that stands for the protection of the privileges of all Americans, whether they be gentiles or Jews or of any creed or religion, or any school of thought that maintains its self-respect for our institutions.

We stand appalled today at what we witness in Europe. Whose heart can fail to become anguished as he reads in the daily press of the terrible abuses and atrocities and indignities and brutalities that are now being inflicted by the German government and some of the German people on the Jews of that nation? One of the most appalling events in history, shameful indeed to our concept of the ethics of our modern civilization which we boast, harking back to the practices of the medieval ages, the torture and debasement of a great race of people who only ask the right to live.

Our Declaration of Independence says that we hold all men to be created equal. That means regardless of his creed, his color, his race, or his nationality. We foregather under that flag and we proclaim that creed, but that principle is being made a mock in the Germany of today. In Germany the labor movement was first wiped out and its leaders were harried and sent to concentration camps, and now, in progressive fury and increasing brutality, the German government is found inflicting these pogroms on the Jewish race.

I say to my fellow countrymen, and I say it to the rich and influential and wealthy gentiles of America as I say it to the rich and influential Jews of America, you cannot strike down in this country through the use of your influence, great as it may be, a powerful movement of the workers of this country under the banner of the CIO, who stand for equality of protection to any group, any minority, any religion that exists here in our country.

The United States of America is under increasing pressure in the realm of foreign affairs. The United States of America may one of these days face a great external crisis. When this mad, bloodthirsty wolf of the German government inflicts its will upon the defenseless people of Germany, of Austria, and of Czechoslovakia, and incites individuals in other countries to perpetrate the same atrocities in Europe, then it is possible that we will have to meet the German dictator as he tries to extend his domain into the realm of the Western Hemisphere.

If that day comes, who is going to sustain the United States of America? Who is going to man its industries? Who is going to send its young men to military ranks to engage in war? Labor — labor! Who is going to protect the institutions of this country, those that are meritorious? Labor! Who is going to protect the titles to property and great wealth down through the generations in America? Labor!

Who is going to do the suffering and the dying in the future but the sons and the daughters of the workers of this country? The workers of this country will never make anything out of war; they merely work and sweat and fight and die. Someone else takes the profits. Who took the profits in the last war? Not labor. And if war comes, the United States needs the cooperation of the millions and millions of workers that are members of the CIO.

In consideration of all of these things, in consideration of the fact that we are Americans and that we believe in the principles of our government, that we are willing to fight at any time to maintain

that flag, we are going to ask from those who are the beneficiaries of that service and that attitude and that policy and that loyalty, we are going to ask proper treatment ourselves — proper treatment ourselves! And I have every confidence that our government and our State Department will make emphatic representations to the German government, protesting the actions of that government in permitting these atrocities to be inflicted on the Jewish people. I say to the government of the United States if, as, and when it takes that action, the 20 million members of the CIO and their dependents will support the government and uphold its hands.

The old order changes. Neither opposition nor misrepresentation is going to destroy the existence of the CIO as a living entity, and the people in high places in America who are now using their influence, through great newspapers and publications, who have opened the sluice gates of adverse propaganda against the CIO in America, will awaken to the fact that their efforts are futile and that the day may come when they, individually, will be rushing to the CIO and begging for its protection for their special privileges and their wealth.

I express to you all my appreciation of your courteous attention while I have made these few remarks. I express with you our hope that from the deliberations of this convention may come renewed inspiration and greater confidence for the millions of workers of this country who are looking to the CIO to give them aid and assistance.

We must not forget that we have 12 million more or less unemployed people in America who have a right to work, but who have not been given work; that there are dependent upon those 12 million many more millions who are underprivileged, ill-provided for, and who are asking for a participation and are looking to this convention to devise policies, to state objectives, to lay out procedure that will cause them to have hope for the future.

I am sure that every man and woman here recognizes the great weight of responsibility upon them in their representative capacities, and that each will contribute toward the successful foundation and the final completion of this great, new, modern labor movement of the CIO.

FRANKLIN D. ROOSEVELT: THE GOOD NEIGHBOR POLICY (1936)

Source: *Peace and War: United States Foreign Policy 1931–1941*, Washington, 1943, pp. 323–329.

Long before I returned to Washington as President of the United States, I had made up my mind that, pending what might be called a more opportune moment on other continents, the United States could best serve the cause of a peaceful humanity by setting an example. That was why on the 4th of March, 1933, I made the following declaration:

In the field of world policy I would dedicate this nation to the policy of the good neighbor — the neighbor who resolutely respects himself and, because he does so, respects the rights of others — the neighbor who respects his obligations and respects the sanctity of his agreements in and with a world of neighbors.

This declaration represents my purpose; but it represents more than a purpose, for it stands for a practice. To a measurable degree it has succeeded; the whole world now knows that the United States cherishes no predatory ambitions. We are strong; but less powerful nations know that they need not fear our strength. We seek no conquest: we stand for peace.

In the whole of the Western Hemisphere our good-neighbor policy has produced results that are especially heartening.

The noblest monument to peace and to neighborly economic and social friendship in all the world is not a monument in bronze or stone, but the boundary which unites the United States and Canada — 3,000 miles of friendship with no barbed wire, no gun or soldier, and no passport on the whole frontier. Mutual trust made that frontier. To extend the same sort of mutual trust throughout the Americas was our aim.

The American republics to the south of us have been ready always to cooperate with the United States on a basis of equality and mutual respect, but before we inaugurated the good-neighbor policy there was among them resentment and fear because certain administrations in Washington had slighted their national pride and their sovereign rights.

In pursuance of the good-neighbor policy, and because in my younger days

I had learned many lessons in the hard school of experience, I stated that the United States was opposed definitely to armed intervention.

We have negotiated a Pan American convention embodying the principle of nonintervention. We have abandoned the Platt Amendment, which gave us the right to intervene in the internal affairs of the Republic of Cuba. We have withdrawn American Marines from Haiti. We have signed a new treaty which places our relations with Panama on a mutually satisfactory basis. We have undertaken a series of trade agreements with other American countries to our mutual commercial profit. At the request of two neighboring republics, I hope to give assistance in the final settlement of the last serious boundary dispute between any of the American nations.

Throughout the Americas the spirit of the good neighbor is a practical and living fact. The twenty-one American republics are not only living together in friendship and in peace — they are united in the determination so to remain.

To give substance to this determination a conference will meet on Dec. 1, 1936, at the capital of our great southern neighbor Argentina, and it is, I know, the hope of all chiefs of state of the Americas that this will result in measures which will banish wars forever from this vast portion of the earth.

Peace, like charity, begins at home; that is why we have begun at home. But peace in the Western world is not all that we seek.

It is our hope that knowledge of the practical application of the good-neighbor policy in this hemisphere will be borne home to our neighbors across the seas.

WENDELL L. WILLKIE: ACCEPTANCE SPEECH (1940)

Source: *This is Wendell Willkie: A Collection of Speeches and Writings on Present-Day Issues*, New York, 1940, pp. 259–280.

No man is so wise as to foresee what the future holds or to lay out a plan for it. No man can guarantee to maintain peace. Peace is not something that a nation can achieve by itself. It also depends on what some other country does. It is neither practical nor desirable to adopt a foreign program committing the United States to future action under unknown circumstances.

The best that we can do is to decide what principle shall guide us.

For me, that principle can be simply defined: In the foreign policy of the United States, as in its domestic policy, I would do everything to defend American democracy and I would refrain from doing anything that would injure it.

We must not permit our emotions — our sympathies or hatreds — to move us from that fixed principle.

For instance, we must not shirk the necessity of preparing our sons to take care of themselves in case the defense of America leads to war. I shall not undertake to analyze the legislation on this subject that is now before Congress, or to examine the intentions of the Administration with regard to it. I concur with many members of my party, that these intentions must be closely watched. Nevertheless, in spite of these considerations, I cannot ask the American people to put their faith in me without recording my conviction that some form of selective service is the only democratic way in which to secure the trained and competent manpower we need for national defense.

Also, in the light of my principle, we must honestly face our relationship with Great Britain. We must admit that the loss of the British Fleet would greatly weaken our defense. This is because the British Fleet has for years controlled the Atlantic, leaving us free to concentrate in the Pacific. If the British Fleet were lost or captured, the Atlantic might be dominated by Germany, a power hostile to our way of life, controlling in that event most of the ships and shipbuilding facilities of Europe.

This would be calamity for us. We might be exposed to attack on the Atlantic. Our defense would be weakened until we could build a navy and air force strong enough to defend both coasts. Also, our foreign trade would be profoundly affected. That trade is vital to our prosperity. But if we had to trade with a Europe dominated by the present German trade policies, we might have to change our methods to some totalitarian form. This is a prospect that any lover of democracy must view with consternation.

The objective of America is in the opposite direction. We must, in the long run, rebuild a world in which we can live and move and do business in the democratic way.

The President of the United States recently said: "We will extend to the opponents of force the material resources of this nation, and at the same time we will harness the use of those resources in order that we ourselves, in the Americas, may have equipment and training equal to the task of any emergency and every defense."

I should like to state that I am in agreement with these two principles, as I understand them — and I don't understand them as implying military involvement in the present hostilities. As an American citizen I am glad to pledge my wholehearted support to the President in whatever action he may take in accordance with these principles.

But I cannot follow the President in his conduct of foreign affairs in this critical time. There have been occasions when many of us have wondered if he is deliberately inciting us to war. I trust that I have made it plain that in the defense of America, and of our liberties, I should not hesitate to stand for war. But like a great many other Americans I saw what war was like at first hand in 1917. I know what war can do to demoralize civil liberties at home. And I believe it to be the first duty of a President to try to maintain peace.

But Mr. Roosevelt has not done this. He has dabbled in inflammatory statements and manufactured panics. Of course, we in America like to speak our minds freely, but this does not mean that at a critical period in history our President should cause bitterness and confusion for the sake of a little political oratory. The President's attacks on foreign powers have been useless and dangerous. He has courted a war for which the country is hopelessly unprepared—and which it emphatically does not want. He has secretly meddled in the affairs of Europe, and he has even unscrupulously encouraged other countries to hope for more help than we are able to give.

"Walk softly and carry a big stick" was the motto of Theodore Roosevelt. It is still good American doctrine for 1940. Under the present administration the country has been placed in the false position of shouting insults and not even beginning to prepare to take the consequences.

But while he has thus been quick to tell other nations what they ought to do, Mr. Roosevelt has been slow to take the American people into his confidence. He has hesitated to report facts, to explain situations, or to define realistic objectives. The confusion in the nation's mind has been largely due to this lack of information from the White House.

If I am elected President, I plan to reverse both of these policies. I should threaten foreign governments only when our country was threatened by them and when I was ready to act; and I should consider our diplomacy as part of the people's business concerning which they were entitled to prompt and frank reports to the limit of practicability.

Candor in these times is the hope of democracy. We must not kid ourselves any longer. We must begin to tell ourselves the truth—right here—and right now.

We have been sitting as spectators of a great tragedy. The action on the stage of history has been relentless. For instance, the French people were just as brave and intelligent as the Germans. Their armies were considered the best in the world. France and her allies won the last war. They possessed all the material resources they needed. They had wealth and reserves of credit all over the earth. Yet the Germans crushed France like an eggshell.

The reason is now clear: The fault lay with France herself. France believed in the forms of democracy and in the idea of freedom. But she failed to put them to use. She forgot that freedom must be dynamic, that it is forever in the process of creating a new world. This was the lesson that we of America had taught to all countries....

We must face a brutal, perhaps, a terrible fact. Our way of life is in competition with Hitler's way of life. This competition is not merely one of armaments. It is a competition of energy against energy, production against production, brains against brains, salesmanship against salesmanship.

In facing it we should have no fear. History shows that our way of life is the stronger way. From it has come more wealth, more industry, more happiness, more human enlightenment than from any other way. Free men are the strongest men.

But we cannot just take this historical fact for granted. We must make it live. If we are to outdistance the totalitarian powers, we must arise to a new life of adventure and discovery. We must make a wider horizon for the human race. It is to that new life that I pledge myself.

I promise, by returning to those same American principles that overcame German autocracy once before, both in business and in war, to outdistance Hitler in any contest he chooses in 1940 or after. And I promise that when we beat him, we shall beat him on our own terms, in our own American way.

The promises of the present administration cannot lead you to victory against Hitler, or against anyone else. This administration stands for principles exactly opposite to mine. It does not preach the doctrine of growth. It preaches the doctrine of division. We are not asked to make more for ourselves. We are asked to divide among ourselves that which we already have. The New Deal doctrine does not seek risk, it seeks safety. Let us call it the "I pass" doctrine. The New Deal dealt it, and refused to make any more bets on the American future.

Why, that is exactly the course France followed to her destruction! Like the Blum government in France, so has our government become entangled in unfruitful adventures. As in France, so here, we have heard talk of class distinctions and of economic groups preying upon other groups. We are told that capital hates labor and labor, capital. We are told that the different kinds of men, whose task it is to build America, are enemies of one another. And I am ashamed to say that some Americans have made political capital of that supposed enmity.

As for me, I want to say here and now that there is no hate in my heart, and that there will be none in my campaign. It is my belief that there is no hate in the hearts of any group of Americans for any other American group—except as the New Dealers seek to put it there for political purposes. I stand for a new companionship in an industrial society.

Of course, if you start, like the New Deal, with the idea that we shall never have many more automobiles or radios, that we cannot develop many new inventions of importance, that our standard of living must remain what it is, the rest of the argument is easy. Since a few people have more than they need and millions have less than they need, it is necessary to redivide the wealth and turn it back from the few to the many.

But this can only make the poor poorer and the rich less rich. It does not really distribute wealth. It distributes poverty.

Because I am a businessman, formerly connected with a large company, the doctrinaires of the opposition have attacked me as an opponent of liberalism. But I was a liberal before many of these men had heard the word, and I fought for many of the reforms of the elder La Follette, Theodore Roosevelt, and Woodrow Wilson before another Roosevelt adopted—and distorted—liberalism.

I learned my liberalism right here at home. From the factories that came into this town many years ago, large fortunes were made by a few individuals, who thereby acquired too much power over our community. Those same forces were at work throughout the rest of the nation. By 1929 the concentration of private power had gone further than it should ever go in a democracy.

We all know that such concentration of power must be checked. Thomas Jefferson disliked regulation, yet he said that the prime purpose of government in a democracy is to keep men from injuring each other. We know from our own experience that the less fortunate or less skillful among us must be protected from encroachment. That is why we support what is known as the liberal point of view. That is why we believe in reform.

I believe that the forces of free enterprise must be regulated. I am opposed to business monopolies. I believe in collective bargaining, by representatives of labor's own free choice, without any interference and in full protection of those obvious rights. I believe in the maintenance of minimum standards for wages and of maximum standards should constantly improve. I believe in the federal regulation of interstate utilities, of securities markets, and of banking. I believe in federal pensions, in adequate old-age benefits, and in unemployment allowances.

I believe that the federal government has a responsibility to equalize the lot of the farmer with that of the manufacturer.

If this cannot be done by parity of prices, other means must be found—with the least possible regimentation of the farmer's affairs. I believe in the encouragement of cooperative buying and selling, and in the full extension of rural electrification.

The purpose of all such measures is indeed to obtain a better distribution of the wealth and earning power of this country. But I do not base my claim to liberalism solely on my faith in such reforms. American liberalism does not consist merely in reforming things. It consists also in making things. The ability to grow, the ability to make things, is the measure of man's welfare on this earth. To be free, man must be creative.

I am a liberal because I believe that in our industrial age there is no limit to the productive capacity of any man. And so I believe that there is no limit to the horizon of the United States.

I say that we must substitute for the philosophy of distributed scarcity the philosophy of unlimited productivity. I stand for the restoration of full production and reemployment by private enterprise in America.

And I say that we must henceforth ask certain questions of every reform, and of every law to regulate business or industry. We must ask: Has it encouraged our industries to produce? Has it created new opportunities for our youth? Will it increase our standard of living? Will it encourage us to open up a new and bigger world?

A reform that cannot meet these tests is not a truly liberal reform. It is an "I pass" reform. It does not tend to strengthen our system, but to weaken it. It exposes us to aggressors, whether economic or military. It encourages class distinctions and hatreds. And it will lead us inevitably, as I believe we are now headed, toward a form of government alien to ours, and a way of life contrary to the way that our parents taught us here in Elwood.

It is from weakness that people reach for dictators and concentrated government power. Only the strong can be free.

FRANKLIN D. ROOSEVELT: THE FOUR FREEDOMS (1941)

Source: Congressional Record, Washington, 77 Cong., 1 Sess., pp. 44–47.

Just as our national policy in internal affairs has been based upon a decent respect for the rights and dignity of all our fellow-men within our gates, so our national policy in foreign affairs has been based on a decent respect for the rights and dignity of all nations, large and small. And the justice of morality must and will win in the end.

Our national policy is this:

First, by an impressive expression of the public will and without regard to partisanship, we are committed to all-inclusive national defense.

Second, by an impressive expression of the public will and without regard to partisanship, we are committed to full support of all those resolute peoples, everywhere, who are resisting aggression and are thereby keeping war away from our Hemisphere. By this support, we express our determination that the democratic cause shall prevail, and we strengthen the defense and security of our own nation.

Third, by an impressive expression of the public will and without regard to partisanship, we are committed to the proposition that principles of morality and considerations for our own security will never permit us to acquiesce in a peace dictated by aggressors and sponsored by appeasers. We know that enduring peace cannot be bought at the cost of other people's freedom.

In the recent national election there was no substantial difference between the two great parties in respect to that national policy. No issue was fought out on this line before the American electorate. Today it is abundantly evident that American citizens everywhere are demanding and supporting speedy and complete action in recognition of obvious danger. Therefore, the immediate need is a swift and driving increase in our armament production.

Leaders of industry and labor have responded to our summons. Goals of speed have been set. In some cases these goals are being reached ahead of time; in some cases we are on schedule; in other cases there are slight but not serious delays; and in some cases—and I am sorry to say very important cases—we are all concerned by the slowness of the accomplishment of our plans. The Army and Navy, however, have made substantial progress during the past year. Actual experience is improving and speeding up our methods of production with every passing day. And today's best is not good enough for tomorrow.

I am not satisfied with the progress thus far made. The men in charge of the program represent the best in training, ability, and patriotism. They are not satisfied with the progress thus far made. None of us will be satisfied until the job is done.

No matter whether the original goal was set too high or too low, our objective is quicker and better results.

To give two illustrations:

We are behind schedule in turning out finished airplanes; we are working day and night to solve the innumerable problems and to catch up.

We are ahead of schedule in building warships; but we are working to get even further ahead of schedule.

To change a whole nation from a basis of peacetime production of implements of peace to a basis of wartime production of implements of war is no small task. And the greatest difficulty comes at the beginning of the program, when new tools and plant facilities and new assembly lines and shipways must first be constructed before the actual material begins to flow steadily and speedily from them.

The Congress, of course, must rightly keep itself informed at all times of the progress of the program. However, there is certain information, as the Congress itself will readily recognize, which, in the interests of our own security and those of the nations we are supporting, must of needs be kept in confidence.

New circumstances are constantly begetting new needs for our safety. I shall ask this Congress for greatly increased new appropriations and authorizations to carry on what we have begun. I also ask this Congress for authority and for funds sufficient to manufacture additional munitions and war supplies of many kinds to be turned over to those nations which are now in actual war with aggressor nations.

Our most useful and immediate role is to act as an arsenal for them as well as for ourselves. They do not need manpower. They do need billions of dollars' worth of the weapons of defense.

The time is near when they will not be able to pay for them in ready cash. We cannot, and will not, tell them they must surrender merely because of present inability to pay for the weapons which we know they must have. I do not recommend that we make them a loan of dollars with which to pay for these weapons—a loan to be repaid in dollars. I recommend that we make it possible for those nations to continue to obtain war materials in the United States, fitting their orders into our own program. Nearly all of their matériel would, if the time ever came, be useful for our own defense.

Taking counsel of expert military and naval authorities, considering what is best for our own security, we are free to decide how much should be kept here and how much should be sent abroad to our friends who, by their determined and heroic resistance, are giving us time in which to make ready our own defense. For what we send abroad we shall be repaid, within a reasonable time following the close of hostilities, in similar materials or, at our option, in other goods of many kinds which they can produce and which we need.

Let us say to the democracies, "We Americans are vitally concerned in your defense of freedom. We are putting forth our energies, our resources, and our organizing powers to give you the strength to regain and maintain a free world. We shall send you, in ever increasing numbers, ships, planes, tanks, guns. This is our purpose and our pledge."

In fulfillment of this purpose we will not be intimidated by the threats of dictators that they will regard as a breach of international law and as an act of war our aid to the democracies which dare to resist their aggression. Such aid is not an act of war, even if a dictator should unilaterally proclaim it so to be. When the dictators are ready to make war upon us, they will not wait for an act of war on our part. They did not wait for Norway or Belgium or the Netherlands to commit an act of war. Their only interest is in a new one-way international law, which lacks mutuality in its observance and, therefore, becomes an instrument of oppression.

The happiness of future generations of Americans may well depend upon how effective and how immediate we can make our aid felt. No one can tell the exact character of the emergency situations that we may be called upon to meet. The nation's hands must not be tied when the nation's life is in danger. We must all prepare to make the sacrifices that the emergency—as serious as war itself—demands. Whatever stands in the way of speed and efficiency in defense preparations must give way to the national need.

A free nation has the right to expect full cooperation from all groups. A free nation has the right to look to the leaders of business, of labor, and of agriculture to take the lead in stimulating effort, not among other groups but within their own groups.

The best way of dealing with the few slackers or troublemakers in our midst is, first, to shame them by patriotic example; and if that fails, to use the sovereignty of government to save government.

As men do not live by bread alone, they do not fight by armaments alone. Those who man our defenses and those behind them who build our defenses must have the stamina and courage which come from an unshakable belief in the manner of life which they are defending. The mighty action which we are calling for cannot be based on a disregard of all things worth fighting for.

The nation takes great satisfaction and much strength from the things which have been done to make its people conscious of their individual stake in the preservation of democratic life in

America. Those things have toughened the fiber of our people, have renewed their faith and strengthened their devotion to the institutions we make ready to protect.

Certainly this is no time to stop thinking about the social and economic problems which are the root cause of the social revolution which is today a supreme factor in the world. There is nothing mysterious about the foundations of a healthy and strong democracy. The basic things expected by our people of their political and economic systems are simple. They are: Equality of opportunity for youth and for others; jobs for those who can work; security for those who need it; the ending of special privilege for the few; the preservation of civil liberties for all; the enjoyment of the fruits of scientific progress in a wider and constantly rising standard of living. These are the simple and basic things that must never be lost sight of in the turmoil and unbelievable complexity of our modern world. The inner and abiding strength of our economic and political systems is dependent upon the degree to which they fulfill these expectations.

Many subjects connected with our social economy call for immediate improvement. As examples:

We should bring more citizens under the coverage of old-age pensions and unemployment insurance.

We should widen the opportunities for adequate medical care.

We should plan a better system by which persons deserving or needing gainful employment may obtain it.

I have called for personal sacrifice. I am assured of the willingness of almost all Americans to respond to that call. A part of the sacrifice means the payment of more money in taxes. In my budget message I recommend that a greater portion of this great defense program be paid for from taxation than we are paying today. No person should try, or be allowed, to get rich out of this program; and the principle of tax payments in accordance with ability to pay should be constantly before our eyes to guide our legislation. If the Congress maintains these principles, the voters, putting patriotism ahead of pocketbooks, will give you their applause.

In the future days, which we seek to make secure, we look forward to a world founded upon four essential human freedoms.

The first is freedom of speech and expression everywhere in the world.

The second is freedom of every person to worship God in his own way everywhere in the world.

The third is freedom from want, which, translated into world terms, means economic understandings which will secure to every nation a healthy peacetime life for its inhabitants everywhere in the world.

The fourth is freedom from fear—which, translated into world terms, means a worldwide reduction of armaments to such a point and in such a thorough fashion that no nation will be in a position to commit an act of physical aggression against any neighbor—anywhere in the world.

That is no vision of a distant millennium. It is a definite basis for a kind of world attainable in our own time and generation. That kind of world is the very antithesis of the so-called new order of tyranny which the dictators seek to create with the crash of a bomb.

To that new order we oppose the greater conception—the moral order. A good society is able to face schemes of world domination and foreign revolutions alike without fear.

Since the beginning of our American history, we have been engaged in change—in a perpetual peaceful revolution—a revolution which goes on steadily, quietly adjusting itself to changing conditions—without the concentration camp or the quicklime in the ditch. The world order which we seek is the cooperation of free countries, working together in a friendly, civilized society.

This nation has placed its destiny in the hands and hearts of its millions of free men and women, and its faith in freedom under the guidance of God. Freedom means the supremacy of human rights everywhere. Our support goes to those who struggle to gain those rights or keep them. Our strength is in our unity of purpose. To that high concept there can be no end save victory.

HUGO BLACK, FELIX FRANKFURTER, FRANK MURPHY, AND ROBERT H. JACKSON: *KOREMATSU V. UNITED STATES* (1944)

Source: United States Reports [Supreme Court], Vol. 323, pp. 214ff.

Mr. Justice Black delivered the opinion of the Court.

The petitioner, an American citizen of Japanese descent, was convicted in a Federal District Court for remaining in San Leandro, California, a "Military Area," contrary to Civilian Exclusion Order No. 34 of the Commanding General of the Western Command, U. S. Army, which directed that after May 9, 1942, all persons of Japanese ancestry should be excluded from that area. No question was raised as to petitioner's loyalty to the United States. The Circuit Court of Appeals affirmed, and the importance of the constitutional question involved caused us to grant certiorari.

It should be noted, to begin with, that all legal restrictions which curtail the civil rights of a single racial group are immediately suspect. That is not to say that all such restrictions are unconstitutional. It is to say that courts must subject them to the most rigid scrutiny. Pressing public necessity may sometimes justify the existence of such restrictions; racial antagonism never can.

In the instant case, prosecution of the petitioner was begun by information charging violation of an Act of Congress, of March 21, 1942, 56 Stat. 173, which provides that:

> *Whoever shall enter, remain in, leave, or commit any act in any military area or military zone prescribed, under the authority of an executive order of the President, by the secretary of war, or by any military commander designated by the secretary of war, contrary to the restrictions applicable to any such area or zone or contrary to the order of the secretary of war or any such military commander, shall, if it appears that he knew or should have known of the existence and extent of the restrictions or order and that his act was in violation thereof, be guilty of a misdemeanor and upon conviction shall be liable to a fine of not to exceed $5,000 or to imprisonment for not more than one year, or both, for each offense.*

Exclusion Order No. 34, which the petitioner knowingly and admittedly violated, was one of a number of military orders and proclamations, all of which were substantially based upon Executive Order No. 9066, 7 Fed. Reg. 1407. That order, issued after we were at war with Japan, declared that "the successful prosecution of the war requires every possible protection against espionage and against sabotage to national-defense material, national-defense premises, and national-defense utilities. ..."

One of the series of orders and proclamations, a curfew order, which, like the exclusion order here was promulgated pursuant to Executive Order 9066, subjected all persons of Japanese ancestry in prescribed West Coast military areas to remains in their residences from 8 p.m. to 6 a.m. As is the case with the exclusion order here, that prior curfew order was designed as a "protection against espionage and against sabotage." In Hirabayashi v. United States, 320 U.S. 81, we sustained a conviction obtained for violation of the curfew order. The Hirabayashi conviction and this one thus rest on the same 1942 congressional act and the same basic executive and military orders, all of which orders were aimed at the twin dangers of espionage and sabotage.

The 1942 act was attacked in the Hirabayashi case as an unconstitutional delegation of power; it was contended that the curfew order and other orders on which it rested were beyond the war powers of the Congress, the military authorities, and of the President, as commander in chief of the Army; and, finally, that to apply the curfew order against none but citizens of Japanese ancestry amounted to a constitutionally prohibited discrimination solely on account of race. To these questions, we gave the serious consideration which their importance justified. We upheld the curfew order as an exercise of the power of the government to take steps necessary to prevent espionage and sabotage in an area threatened by Japanese attack.

In the light of the principles we announced in the Hirabayashi case, we are unable to conclude that it was beyond the war power of Congress and the executive to exclude those of Japanese ancestry from the West Coast war area at the time they did. True, exclusion from the area in which one's home is located is a far greater deprivation than constant confinement to the home from 8 p.m. to 6 a.m. Nothing short of apprehension by the proper military authorities of the gravest imminent danger to the public safety can constitutionally justify either. But exclusion from a threatened area, no less than curfew, has a definite and close relationship to the prevention of espionage and sabotage. The military authorities, charged with the primary responsibility of defending our shores, concluded that curfew provided inadequate protection and ordered exclusion. They did so, as pointed out in our Hirabayashi opinion, in accordance with congressional authority to the military to say who should and who should not remain in the threatened areas.

In this case the petitioner challenges the assumptions upon which we rested our conclusions in the Hirabayashi case. He also urges that by May 1942, when Order No. 34 was promulgated, all danger of Japanese invasion of the West Coast had disappeared. After careful consideration of these contentions, we are compelled to reject them.

Here, as in the Hirabayashi case, supra, at p. 99,

We cannot reject as unfounded the judgment of the military authorities and of Congress that there were disloyal members of that population, whose number and strength could not be precisely and quickly ascertained. We cannot say that the warmaking branches of the government did not have ground for believing that in a critical hour such persons could not readily be isolated and separately dealt with, and constituted a menace to the national defense and safety, which demanded that prompt and adequate measures be taken to guard against it. ...

It is said that we are dealing here with the case of imprisonment of a citizen in a concentration camp solely because of his ancestry, without evidence or inquiry concerning his loyalty and good disposition toward the United States. Our task would be simple, our duty clear, were this a case involving the imprisonment of a loyal citizen in a concentration camp because of racial prejudice. Regardless of the true nature of the assembly and relocation centers — and we deem it unjustifiable to call them concentration camps with all the ugly connotations that term implies — we are dealing specifically with nothing but an exclusion order. To cast this case into outlines of racial prejudice, without reference to the real military dangers which were presented, merely confuses the issue.

Korematsu was not excluded from the Military Area because of hostility to him or his race. He was excluded because we are at war with the Japanese Empire, because the properly constituted military authorities feared an invasion of our West Coast and felt constrained to take proper security measures, because they decided that the military urgency of the situation demanded that all citizens of Japanese ancestry be segregated from the West Coast temporarily, and, finally, because Congress, reposing its confidence in this time of war in our military leaders—as inevitably it must—determined that they should have the power to do just this.

There was evidence of disloyalty on the part of some, the military authorities considered that the need for action was great, and time was short. We cannot—by availing ourselves of the calm perspective of hindsight—now say that at that time these actions were unjustified.

Mr. Justice Frankfurter, concurring.

According to my reading of Civilian Exclusion Order No. 34, it was an offense for Korematsu to be found in Military Area No. 1, the territory wherein he was previously living, except within the bounds of the established Assembly Center of that area. Even though the various orders issued by General DeWitt be deemed a comprehensive code of instructions, their tenor is clear and not contradictory. They put upon Korematsu the obligation to leave Military Area No. 1, but only by the method prescribed in the instructions, i.e., by reporting to the Assembly Center. I am unable to see how the legal considerations that led to the decision in Hirabayashi v. United States, 320 U.S. 81, fail to sustain the military order which made the conduct now in controversy a crime. And so I join in the opinion of the Court, but should like to add a few words of my own.

The provisions of the Constitution which confer on the Congress and the President powers to enable this country to wage war are as much part of the Constitution as provisions looking to a nation at peace. And we have had recent occasion to quote approvingly the statement of former Chief Justice Hughes that the war power of the government is "the power to wage war successfully." Hirabayashi v. United States, supra at 93; and see Home Bldg. & L. Assn. v. Blaisdell, 290 U.S. 398, 426. Therefore, the validity of action under the war power must be judged wholly in the context of war. That action is not to be stigmatized as lawless because like action in times of peace would be lawless. To talk about a military order that expresses an allowable judgment of war needs by those entrusted with the duty of conducting war as "an unconstitutional order" is to suffuse a part of the Constitution with an atmosphere of unconstitutionality.

The respective spheres of action of military authorities and of judges are of course very different. But within their sphere, military authorities are no more outside the bounds of obedience to the Constitution than are judges within theirs. "The war power of the United States, like its other powers ... is subject to applicable constitutional limitations," Hamilton v. Kentucky Distilleries Co., 251 U.S. 146, 156. To recognize that military orders are "reasonably expedient military precautions" in time of war and yet to deny them constitutional legitimacy makes of the Constitution an instrument for dialectic subleties not reasonably to be attributed to the hard-headed framers, of whom a majority had had actual participation in war.

If a military order such as that under review does not transcend the means appropriate for conducting war, such action by the military is as constitutional as would be any authorized action by the Interstate Commerce Commission within the limits of the constitutional power to regulate commerce. And being an exercise of the war power explicitly granted by the Constitution for safeguarding the national life by prosecuting war effectively, I find nothing in the Constitution which denies to Congress the power to enforce such a valid military order by making its violation an offense triable in the civil courts. Compare Interstate Commerce Commission v. Brimson, 154 U.S. 447; 155 U.S. 3, and Monongahela Bridge Co. v. United States, 216 U.S. 177. To find that the Constitution does not forbid the military measures now complained of does not carry with it approval of that which Congress and the executive did. That is their business, not ours.

Mr. Justice Murphy, dissenting.

It must be conceded that the military and naval situation in the spring of 1942 was such as to generate a very real fear of invasion of the Pacific Coast, accompanied by fears of sabotage and espionage in that area. The military command was therefore justified in adopting all reasonable means necessary to combat these dangers. In adjudging the military action taken in light of the then apparent dangers, we must not erect too high or too meticulous standards; it is necessary only that the action have some reasonable relation to the removal of the dangers of invasion, sabotage, and espionage. But the exclusion, either temporarily or permanently, of all persons with Japanese blood in their veins has no such reasonable relation. And that relation is lacking because the exclusion order necessarily must rely for its reasonableness upon the assumption that all persons of Japanese ancestry may have a dangerous tendency to commit sabotage and espionage and to aid our Japanese enemy in other ways. It is difficult to believe that reason, logic, or experience could be marshaled in support of such an assumption.

That this forced exclusion was the result in good measure of this erroneous assumption of racial guilt rather than bona fide military necessity is evidenced by the Commanding General's Final Report on the evacuation from the Pacific Coast area. In it he refers to all individuals of Japanese descent as "subversive," as belonging to "an enemy race" whose "racial strains are undiluted," and as constituting "over 112,000 potential enemies ... at large today" along the Pacific Coast. In support of this blanket condemnation of all persons of Japanese descent, however, no reliable evidence is cited to show that such individuals were generally disloyal, or had generally so conducted themselves in this area as to constitute a special menace to defense installations or war industries, or had otherwise by their behavior furnished reasonable ground for their exclusion as a group.

Justification for the exclusion is sought, instead, mainly upon questionable racial and sociological grounds not ordinarily within the realm of expert military judgment, supplemented by certain semi-military conclusions drawn from an unwarranted use of circumstantial evidence. Individuals of Japanese ancestry are condemned because they are said to be "a large, unassimilated, tightly knit racial group, bound to an enemy nation by strong ties of race, culture, custom and religion." They are claimed to be given to "emperor-worshiping ceremonies" and to "dual citizenship." Japanese language schools and allegedly pro-Japanese organizations are cited as evidence of possible group disloyalty, together with facts as to certain persons being educated and residing at length in Japan. It is intimated that many of these individuals deliberately resided "adjacent to strategic points," thus enabling them "to carry into execution a tremendous program of sabotage on a mass scale should any considerable number of them have been inclined to do so."

The need for protective custody is also asserted. The report refers without identity to "numerous incidents of violence" as well as to other admittedly unverified or cumulative incidents. From this, plus certain other events not shown to have been connected with the Japanese Americans, it is concluded that the "situation was fraught with danger to the Japanese population itself" and that the general public "was ready to take matters into its own hands." Finally, it is intimated, though not directly charged or proved, that persons of Japanese ancestry were responsible for three minor isolated shellings and bombings of the Pacific Coast area, as well as for unidentified radio transmissions and night signaling.

The main reasons relied upon by those responsible for the forced evacuation, therefore, do not prove a reasonable relation between the group characteristics of Japanese Americans and the dangers of invasion, sabotage, and espionage. The reasons appear, instead, to be largely an accumulation of much of the misinformation, half-truths, and insinuations that for years have been directed against Japanese Americans by people with racial and economic prejudices—the same people who have been among the foremost advocates of the evacuation. A military judgment based upon such racial and sociological considerations is not entitled to the great weight ordinarily given the judgments based upon strictly military considerations. Especially is this so when every charge relative to race, religion, culture, geographical location, and legal and economic status has been substantially discredited by independent studies made by experts in these matters.

The military necessity which is essential to the validity of the evacuation order thus resolves itself into a few intimations that certain individuals actively aided the enemy, from which it is inferred that the entire group of Japanese Americans could not be trusted to be or remain loyal to the United States. ...

No adequate reason is given for the failure to treat these Japanese Americans on an individual basis by holding investigations and hearings to separate the loyal from the disloyal, as was done in the case of persons of German and Italian ancestry. See House Report No. 2124 (77th Cong., 2d Sess.) 247–52. It is asserted merely that the loyalties of this group "were unknown and time was of the essence." Yet nearly four months elapsed after Pearl Harbor before the first exclusion order was issued; nearly eight months went by until the last order was issued; and the last of these "subversive" persons was not actually removed until almost eleven months had elapsed. Leisure and deliberation seem to have been more of the essence than speed. And the fact that conditions were not such as to warrant a declaration of martial law adds strength to the belief that the factors of time and military necessity were not as urgent as they have been represented to be.

Moreover, there was no adequate proof that the Federal Bureau of Investigation and the military and naval intelligence services did not have the espionage and sabotage situation well in hand during this long period. Nor is there any denial of the fact that not one person of Japanese ancestry was accused or convicted of espionage or sabotage after Pearl Harbor while they were still free, a fact which is some evidence of the loyalty of the vast majority of these individuals and of the effectiveness of the established methods of combatting these evils. It seems incredible that under these circumstances it would have been impossible to hold loyalty hearings for the mere 112,000 persons involved—or at least for the 70,000 American citizens—especially when a large part of this number represented children and elderly men and women. Any inconvenience that may have accompanied an attempt to conform to procedural due process cannot be said to justify violations of constitutional rights of individuals.

I dissent, therefore, from this legalization of racism. Racial discrimination in any form and in any degree has no justifiable part whatever in our democratic way of life. It is unattractive in any setting but it is utterly revolting among a free people who have embraced the principles set forth in the Constitution of the United States. All residents of this nation are kin in some way by blood or culture to a foreign land. Yet they are primarily and necessarily a part of the new and distinct civilization of the United States. They must accordingly be treated at all times as the heirs of the American experiment and as entitled to all the rights and freedoms guaranteed by the Constitution.

Mr. Justice Jackson, dissenting.

Korematsu was born on our soil, of parents born in Japan. The Constitution makes him a citizen of the United States by nativity and a citizen of California by residence. No claim is made that he is not loyal to this country. There is no suggestion that apart from the matter involved here he is not law-abiding and well disposed. Korematsu, however, has been convicted of an act not commonly a crime. It consists merely of being present in the state whereof he is a citizen, near the place where he was born, and where all his life he has lived.

Even more unusual is the series of military orders which made this conduct a crime. They forbid such a one to remain, and they also forbid him to leave. They were so drawn that the only way Korematsu could avoid violation was to give himself up to the military authority. This meant submission to custody, examination, and transportation out of the territory, to be followed by indeterminate confinement in detention camps.

A citizen's presence in the locality, however, was made a crime only if his parents were of Japanese birth. Had Korematsu been one of four — the others being, say, a German alien enemy, an Italian alien enemy, and a citizen of American-born ancestors convicted of treason but out on parole — only Korematsu's presence would have violated the order. The difference between their innocence and his crime would result, not from anything he did, said, or thought different than they but only in that he was born of different racial stock.

Now, if any fundamental assumption underlies our system, it is that guilt is personal and not inheritable. Even if all of one's antecedents had been convicted of treason, the Constitution forbids its penalties to be visited upon him, for it provides that "no attainder of treason shall work corruption of blood or forfeiture except during the life of the person attainted." But here is an attempt to make an otherwise innocent act a crime merely because this prisoner is the son of parents as to whom he had no choice and belongs to a race from which there is no way to resign. If Congress in peacetime legislation should enact such a criminal law, I should suppose this Court would refuse to enforce it.

But the "law" which this prisoner is convicted of disregarding is not found in an act of Congress but in a military order. Neither the act of Congress nor the executive order of the President, nor both together, would afford a basis for this conviction. It rests on the orders of General DeWitt. And it is said that if the military commander had reasonable military grounds for promulgating the orders, they are constitutional and become law, and the Court is required to enforce them. There are several reasons why I cannot subscribe to this doctrine.

It would be impracticable and dangerous idealism to expect or insist that each specific military command in an area of probable operations will conform to conventional tests of constitutionality. When an area is so beset that it must be put under military control at all, the paramount consideration is that its measures be successful rather than legal. The armed services must protect a society, not merely its Constitution. The very essence of the military job is to marshal physical force, to remove every obstacle to its effectiveness, to give it every strategic advantage. Defense measures will not, and often should not, be held within the limits that bind civil authority in peace. No court can require such a commander in such circumstances to act as a reasonable man; he may be unreasonably cautious and exacting. Perhaps he should be. But a commander in temporarily focusing the life of a community on defense is carrying out a military program; he is not making law in the sense the courts know the term. He issues orders, and they may have a certain authority as military commands, although they may be very bad as constitutional law.

But if we cannot confine military expedients by the Constitution, neither would I distort the Constitution to approve all that the military may deem expedient. That is what the Court appears to be doing, whether consciously or not. I cannot say, from any evidence before me, that the orders of General DeWitt were not reasonably expedient military precautions, nor could I say that they were. But even if they were permissible military procedures, I deny that it follows that they are constitutional. If, as the Court holds, it does follow, then we may as well say that any military order will be constitutional and have done with it. ...

A military order, however unconstitutional, is not apt to last longer than the military emergency. Even during that period a succeeding commander may revoke it all. But once a judicial opinion rationalizes such an order to show that it conforms to the Constitution, or rather rationalizes the Constitution to show that the Constitution sanctions such an order, the Court for all time has validated the principle of racial discrimination in criminal procedure and of transplanting American citizens. The principle then lies about like a loaded weapon ready for the hand of any authority that can bring forward a plausible claim of an urgent need. Every repetition imbeds that principle more deeply in our law and thinking and expands it to new purposes. All who observe the work of courts are familiar with what Judge Cardozo described as "the tendency of a principle to expand itself to the limit of its logic." A military commander may overstep the bounds of constitutionality and it is an incident. But if we review and approve, that passing incident becomes the doctrine of the Constitution. There it has a generative power of its own, and all that it creates will be in its own image. Nothing better illustrates this danger than does the Court's opinion in this case. ...

I should hold that a civil court cannot be made to enforce an order which violates constitutional limitations even if it is a reasonable exercise of military authority. The courts can exercise only the judicial power, can apply only law, and must abide by the Constitution, or they cease to be civil courts and become instruments of military policy.

THE YALTA AGREEMENT (1945)

Source: [United States Department of State] Papers Relating to Foreign Relations of the United States, Washington, Department of State Publication 6199: "The Conferences at Malta and Yalta 1945."

The Crimea Conference of the heads of the governments of the United States of America, the United Kingdom, and the Union of Soviet Socialist Republics which took place from February 4 to 11 came to the following conclusions.

I. World Organization

It was decided:

- That a United Nations Conference on the proposed world organization should be summoned for Wednesday, 25 April, 1945, and should be held in the United States of America.
- The nations to be invited to this conference should be:
  (a) the United Nations as they existed on the 8 February, 1945, and
  (b) such of the Associated Nations as have declared war on the common enemy by 1 March, 1945. (For this purpose by the term "Associated Nation" was meant the eight Associated Nations and Turkey.) When the Conference on World Organization is held, the delegates of the United Kingdom and United States of America will support a proposal to admit to original membership two Soviet Socialist republics, i.e., the Ukraine and White Russia.
- That the United States government on behalf of the Three Powers should consult the government of China and the French Provisional Government in regard to the decisions taken at the present conference concerning the proposed world organization.
- That the text of the invitation to be issued to all the nations which would take part in the United Nations Conference should be as follows:

Invitation

The government of the United States of America, on behalf of itself and of the governments of the United Kingdom, the Union of Soviet Socialist Republics, and the Republic of China and of the Provisional Government of the French Republic, invite the government of ——— to send representatives to a Conference of the United Nations to be held on 25 April, 1945, or soon thereafter, at San Francisco in the United States of America to prepare a charter for a general international organization for the maintenance of international peace and security.

The above-named governments suggest that the conference consider as affording a basis for such a charter the proposals for the establishment of a general international organization which were made public last October as a result of the Dumbarton Oaks Conference, and which have now been supplemented by the following provisions for Section C of Chapter VI:

C. Voting

- Each member of the Security Council should have one vote.
- Decisions of the Security Council on procedural matters should be made by an affirmative vote of seven members.
- Decisions of the Security Council on all other matters should be made by an affirmative vote of seven members, including the concurring votes of the permanent members; provided that, in decisions under Chapter VIII, Section A, and under the second sentence of paragraph 1 of Chapter VIII, Section C, a party to a dispute should abstain from voting.

Further information as to arrangements will be transmitted subsequently.

In the event that the government of ——— desires in advance of the conference to present views or comments concerning the proposals, the government of the United States of America will be pleased to transmit such views and comments to the other participating governments.

Territorial Trusteeship

It was agreed that the five nations which will have permanent seats on the Security Council should consult each other prior to the United Nations Conference on the question of territorial trusteeship.

The acceptance of this recommendation is subject to its being made clear that territorial trusteeship will only apply to (a) existing mandates of the League of Nations; (b) territories detached from the enemy as a result of the present war; (c) any other territory which might voluntarily be placed under trusteeship; and (d) no discussion of actual territories is contemplated at the forthcoming United Nations Conference or in the preliminary consultations, and it will be a matter for subsequent agreement which territories within the above categories will be placed under trusteeship.

II. DECLARATION ON LIBERATED EUROPE

The following declaration has been approved:

The Premier of the Union of Soviet Socialist Republics, the Prime Minister of the United Kingdom, and the President of the United States of America have consulted with each other in the common interests of the peoples of their countries and those of liberated Europe. They jointly declare their mutual agreement to concert during the temporary period of instability in liberated Europe the policies of their three governments in assisting the peoples liberated from the domination of Nazi Germany and the peoples of the former Axis satellite states of Europe to solve by democratic means their pressing political and economic problems.

The establishment of order in Europe and the rebuilding of national economic life must be achieved by processes which will enable the liberated peoples to destroy the last vestiges of Nazism and Fascism and to create democratic institutions of their own choice. This is a principle of the Atlantic Charter — the right of all peoples to choose the form of government under which they will live — the restoration of sovereign rights and self-government to those peoples who have been forcibly deprived of them by the aggressor nations.

To foster the conditions in which the liberated peoples may exercise these rights, the three governments will jointly assist the people in any European liberated state or former Axis satellite state in Europe where in their judgment conditions require (a) to establish conditions of internal peace; (b) to carry out emergency measures for the relief of distressed peoples; (c) to form interim governmental authorities broadly representative of all democratic elements in the population and pledged to the earliest possible establishment through free elections of governments responsive to the will of the people; and (d) to facilitate where necessary the holding of such elections.

The three governments will consult the other United Nations and provisional authorities or other governments in Europe when matters of direct interest to them are under consideration.

When, in the opinion of the three governments, conditions in any European liberated state or any former Axis satellite state in Europe make such action necessary, they will immediately consult together on the measures necessary to discharge the joint responsibilities set forth in this declaration.

By this declaration we reaffirm our faith in the principles of the Atlantic Charter, our pledge in the Declaration by the United Nations, and our determination to build in cooperation with other peace-loving nations world order under law, dedicated to peace, security, freedom, and general well-being of all mankind.

In issuing this declaration, the Three Powers express the hope that the Provisional Government of the French Republic may be associated with them in the procedure suggested.

III. Dismemberment of Germany

It was agreed that Article 12 (a) of the Surrender Terms for Germany should be amended to read as follows:

The United Kingdom, the United States of America, and the Union of Soviet Socialist Republics shall possess supreme authority with respect to Germany. In the exercise of such authority they will take such steps, including the complete disarmament, demilitarization, and the dismemberment of Germany as they deem requisite for future peace and security.

The study of the procedure for the dismemberment of Germany was referred to a committee consisting of Mr. Eden (chairman), Mr. Winant, and Mr. Gousev. This body would consider the desirability of associating with it a French representative.

IV. ZONE OF OCCUPATION FOR THE FRENCH AND CONTROL COUNCIL FOR GERMANY

It was agreed that a zone in Germany, to be occupied by the French forces, should be allocated to France. This zone would be formed out of the British and American zones and its extent would be settled by the British and Americans in consultation with the French Provisional Government.

It was also agreed that the French Provisional Government should be invited to become a member of the Allied Control Council for Germany.

V. REPARATION

The following protocol has been approved:

- Germany must pay in kind for the losses caused by her to the Allied Nations in the course of the war. Reparations are to be received in the first instance by those countries which have borne the main burden of the war, have suffered the heaviest losses, and have organized victory over the enemy.

- Reparation in kind is to be exacted from Germany in three following forms:

(a) Removals within two years from the surrender of Germany or the cessation of organized resistance from the national wealth of Germany located on the territory of Germany herself, as well as outside her territory (equipment, machine tools, ships, rolling stock, German investments abroad, shares of industrial, transport, and other enterprises in Germany, etc.), these removals to be carried out chiefly for purpose of destroying the war potential of Germany.

(b) Annual deliveries of goods from current production for a period to be fixed.

(c) Use of German labor.

- For the working out on the above principles of a detailed plan for exaction of reparation from Germany, an Allied Reparation Commission will be set up in Moscow. cow. It will consist of three representatives — one from the Union of Soviet Socialist Republics, one from the United Kingdom, and one from the United States of America.

- With regard to the fixing of the total sum of the reparation as well as the distribution of it among the countries which suffered from the German aggression, the Soviet and American delegations agreed as follows:

The Moscow Reparation Commission should take in its initial studies as a basis for discussion the suggestion of the Soviet government that the total sum of the reparation in accordance with the points (a) and (b) of the paragraph 2 should be $20 billion and that 50 percent of it should go to the Union of Soviet Socialist Republics.

The British delegation was of the opinion that pending consideration of the reparation question by the Moscow Reparation Commission no figures of reparation should be mentioned.

The above Soviet-American proposal has been passed to the Moscow Reparation Commission as one of the proposals to be considered by the Commission.

VI. Major War Criminals

The Conference agreed that the question of the major war criminals should be the subject of inquiry by the three foreign secretaries for report in due course after the close of the conference.

VII. Poland

The following Declaration on Poland was agreed by the conference:

A new situation has been created in Poland as a result of her complete liberation by the Red Army. This calls for the establishment of a Polish Provisional Government which can be more broadly based than was possible before the recent liberation of the western part of Poland. The Provisional Government which is now functioning in Poland should therefore be reorganized on a broader democratic basis with the inclusion of democratic leaders from Poland itself and from Poles abroad. This new government should then be called the Polish Provisional Government of National Unity.

M. Molotov, Mr. Harriman, and Sir A. Clark Kerr are authorized as a commission to consult in the first instance in Moscow with members of the present Provisional Government and with other Polish democratic leaders from within Poland and from abroad, with a view to the reorganization of the present government along the above lines. This Polish Provisional Government of National Unity shall be pledged to the holding of free and unfettered elections as soon as possible on the basis of universal suffrage and secret ballot. In these elections all democratic and anti-Nazi parties shall have the right to take part and to put forward candidates.

When a Polish Provisional Government of National Unity has been properly formed in conformity with the above, the government of the U.S.S.R., which now maintains diplomatic relations with the present Provisional Government of Poland, and the government of the United Kingdom and the government of the U.S.A. will establish diplomatic relations with the new Polish Provisional Government of National Unity, and will exchange ambassadors by whose reports the respective governments will be kept informed about the situation in Poland.

The three heads of government consider that the eastern frontier of Poland should follow the Curzon Line, with digressions from it in some regions of five to eight kilometers in favor of Poland. They recognize that Poland must receive substantial accessions of territory in the north and west. They feel that the opinion of the new Polish Provisional Government of National Unity should be sought in due course on the extent of these accessions and that the final delimitation of the western frontier of Poland should thereafter await the Peace Conference.

VIII. YUGOSLAVIA

It was agreed to recommend to Marshal Tito and to Dr. Subasic:

- That the Tito-Subasic Agreement should immediately be put into effect and a new government formed on the basis of the agreement.
- That as soon as the new government has been formed it should declare:

(a) that the Anti-Fascist Assembly of National Liberation (AUNOJ) will be extended to include members of the last Yugoslav Skupstina who have not compromised themselves by collaboration with the enemy, thus forming a body to be known as a temporary parliament and

(b) that legislative acts passed by the Anti-Fascist Assembly of National Liberation (AUNOJ) will be subject to subsequent ratification by a constituent assembly. And that this statement should be published in the communique of the conference.

IX. ITALO-YUGOSLAV FRONTIER; ITALO-AUSTRIA FRONTIER

Notes on these subjects were put in by the British delegation and the American and Soviet delegations agreed to consider them and give their views later.

X. YUGOSLAV-BULGARIAN RELATIONS

There was an exchange of views between the foreign secretaries on the question of the desirability of a Yugoslav-Bulgarian pact of alliance. The question at issue was whether a state still under an armistice regime could be allowed to enter into a treaty with another state. Mr. Eden suggested that the Bulgarian and Yugoslav governments should be informed that this could not be approved. Mr. Stettinius suggested that the British and American ambassadors should discuss the matter further with M. Molotov in Moscow. M. Molotov agreed with the proposal of Mr. Stettinius.

XI. Southeastern Europe

The British delegation put in notes for the consideration of their colleagues on the following subjects:

(a) the Control Commission in Bulgaria
(b) Greek claims upon Bulgaria, more particularly with reference to reparations.
(c) Oil equipment in Rumania.

XII. Iran

Mr. Eden, Mr. Stettinius, and M. Molotov exchanged views on the situation in Iran. It was agreed that this matter should be pursued through the diplomatic channel.

XIII. Meetings of the Three Foreign Secretaries

The conference agreed that the permanent machinery should be set up for consultation between the three foreign secretaries; they should meet as often as necessary, probably about every three or four months. These meetings will be held in rotation in the three capitals, the first meeting being held in London.

XIV. The Montreux Convention and the Straits

It was agreed that at the next meeting of the three foreign secretaries to be held in London they should consider proposals which it was understood the Soviet government would put forward in relation to the Montreux Convention and report to their governments. The Turkish government should be informed at the appropriate moment.

HARRY S. TRUMAN: ANNOUNCEMENT OF THE DROPPING OF AN ATOMIC BOMB ON HIROSHIMA (1945)

Source: Public Papers of the Presidents of the United States: Harry S. Truman, Containing the Public Messages, Speeches, and Statements of the President, April 12 to December 31, 1945, Washington, 1961, pp. 197–200.

Sixteen hours ago an American airplane dropped one bomb on Hiroshima, an important Japanese Army base. That bomb had more power than 20,000 tons of TNT. It had more than 2,000 times the blast power of the British "Grand Slam," which is the largest bomb ever yet used in the history of warfare.

The Japanese began the war from the air at Pearl Harbor. They have been repaid manyfold. And the end is not yet. With this bomb we have now added a new and revolutionary increase in destruction to supplement the growing power of our armed forces. In their present from these bombs are now in production, and even more powerful forms are in development.

It is an atomic bomb. It is a harnessing of the basic power of the universe. The force from which the sun draws its power has been loosed against those who brought war to the Far East.

Before 1939, it was the accepted belief of scientists that it was theoretically possible to release atomic energy. But no one knew any practical method of doing it. By 1942, however, we knew that the Germans were working feverishly to find a way to add atomic energy to the other engines of war with which they hoped to enslave the world. But they failed. We may be grateful to Providence that the Germans got the V-1's and V-2's late and in limited quantities and even more grateful that they did not get the atomic bomb at all.

The battle of the laboratories held fateful risks for us as well as the battles of the air, land, and sea, and we have now won the battle of the laboratories as we have won the other battles.

Beginning in 1940, before Pearl Harbor, scientific knowledge useful in war was pooled between the United States and Great Britain, and many priceless helps to our victories have come from that arrangement. Under that general policy the research on the atomic bomb was begun. With American and British scientists working together we entered the race of discovery against the Germans.

The United States had available the large number of scientists of distinction in the many needed areas of knowledge. It had the tremendous industrial and financial resources necessary for the project, and they could be devoted to it without undue impairment of other vital war work. In the United States the laboratory work and the production plants, on which a substantial start had already been made, would be out of reach of enemy bombing, while at that time Britain was exposed to constant air attack and was still threatened with the possibility of invasion. For these reasons Prime Minister Churchill and President Roosevelt agreed that it was wise to carry on the project here.

We now have two great plants and many lesser works devoted to the production of atomic power. Employment during peak construction numbered 125,000 and over 65,000 individuals are even now engaged in operating the plants. Many have worked there for two and a half years. Few know what they have been producing. They see great quantities of material going in and they see nothing coming out of these plants, for the physical size of the explosive charge is exceedingly small. We have spent $2 billion on the greatest scientific gamble in history—and won.

But the greatest marvel is not the size of the enterprise, its secrecy, nor its cost, but the achievement of scientific brains in putting together infinitely complex pieces of knowledge held by many men in different fields of science into a workable plan. And hardly less marvelous has been the capacity of industry to design, and of labor to operate, the machines and methods to do things never done before so that the brainchild of many minds came forth in physical shape and performed as it was supposed to do. Both science and industry worked under the direction of the United States Army, which achieved a unique success in managing so diverse a problem in the advancement of knowledge in an amazingly short time. It is doubtful if such another combination could be got together in the world. What has been done is the greatest achievement of organized science in history. It was done under high pressure and without failure.

We are now prepared to obliterate more rapidly and completely every productive enterprise the Japanese have above ground in any city. We shall destroy their docks, their factories, and their communications. Let there be no mistake; we shall completely destroy Japan's power to make war.

It was to spare the Japanese people from utter destruction that the ultimatum of July 26 was issued at Potsdam. Their leaders promptly rejected that ultimatum. If they do not now accept our terms they may expect a rain of ruin from the air, the like of which has never been seen on this earth. Behind this air attack will follow sea and land forces in such numbers and power as they have not yet seen and with the

fighting skill of which they are already well aware.

The secretary of war, who has kept in personal touch with all phases of the project, will immediately make public a statement giving further details.

His statement will give facts concerning the sites at Oak Ridge near Knoxville, Tennessee, and at Richland near Pasco, Washington, and an installation near Santa Fe, New Mexico. Although the workers at the sites have been making materials to be used in producing the greatest destructive force in history, they have not themselves been in danger beyond that of many other occupations, for the utmost care has been taken of their safety.

The fact that we can release atomic energy ushers in a new era in man's understanding of nature's forces. Atomic energy may in the future supplement the power that now comes from coal, oil, and falling water, but at present it cannot be produced on a basis to compete with them commercially. Before that comes there must be a long period of intensive research.

It has never been the habit of the scientists of this country or the policy of this government to withhold from the world scientific knowledge. Normally, therefore, everything about the work with atomic energy would be made public.

But under present circumstances it is not intended to divulge the technical processes of production or all the military applications, pending further examination of possible methods of protecting us and the rest of the world from the danger of sudden destruction.

I shall recommend that the Congress of the United States consider promptly the establishment of an appropriate commission to control the production and use of atomic power within the United States. I shall give further consideration and make further recommendations to the Congress as to how atomic power can become a powerful and forceful influence towards the maintenance of world peace.

GLOSSARY

annuity A sum of money paid at regular intervals.

Anti-Saloon League The leading organization lobbying for prohibition in the United States in the early 20th century. Founded as a state society in Ohio in 1893, its influence spread rapidly and in 1895 it became a national organization.

antitrust law Any law restricting business practices that are considered unfair or monopolistic.

audit Examination of the records and reports of an enterprise by accounting specialists other than those responsible for their preparation.

bituminous coal The most abundant form of coal, it has long been used for steam generation in electric power plants and industrial boiler plants.

Bolshevism The doctrine or program of the Bolsheviks advocating violent overthrow of the political and economic institutions of capitalism and the establishment of a socialist state controlled by the workers.

bootlegging Illegal traffic in liquor in the United States.

capitalism An economic system in which most of the means of production are privately owned and production is guided and income distributed largely through the operation of markets.

certiorari A written document issued by a superior court for the reexamination of an action of a lower court.

chantey A song sung by sailors in rhythm with their work.

communism The political and economic doctrine that aims to replace private property and a profit-based economy with public ownership and communal control of at least the major means of production.

cynosure A centre of attraction or attention.

depression A major downswing in the business cycle that is characterized by sharply reduced industrial production, widespread unemployment, serious declines or cessations of growth in construction activity, and great reductions in international trade and capital movements.

disarmament The reduction of a military establishment to a minimum set by some specified authority, or by general international agreement.

exigency A state of affairs that makes urgent demands.

fascism A political philosophy, movement, or regime (as that of the Fascisti in Italy in 1922-43) that exalts nation and often race above the individual and that stands for a centralized autocratic government headed by a dictatorial leader, severe economic and social regimentation, and forcible suppression of opposition.

fundamentalism A movement in 20th century Protestantism emphasizing the literally interpreted Bible as fundamental to Christian life and teaching.

International Monetary Fund A specialized agency of the United Nations founded in 1945 designed to help ensure the smooth international buying and selling of currency. By the early 21st century more than 180 countries were members of the IMF.

isolationism A policy of national isolation by abstention from alliances and other international political and economic relations.

jalopy A dilapidated old vehicle (as an automobile).

Ku Klux Klan Either of two distinct U.S. hate organizations that have employed terror in pursuit of their white supremacist agenda. One group was founded immediately after the Civil War and lasted until the 1870s; the other began in 1915 and has continued to the present.

margin A percentage of a loan that must be paid as a down payment by an investor buying on credit. This percentage, which is paid on top of the loan amount, is so named as it provides a "margin" of safety to the lender.

moratorium A legally authorized period of delay in the performance of a legal obligation or the payment of a debt.

muckraker One who searches out and publicly exposes real or apparent misconduct of a prominent individual or business.

munition Ammunition, weapons, and all supplies used in war for direct military action.

open shop An establishment in which eligibility for employment and retention on the payroll requires neither membership in a labour union membership nor dues payment. There may, however, be an agreement by which a union is recognized as sole bargaining agent.

parity An equivalence between farmers' current purchasing power and their purchasing power at a selected base period maintained by government support of agricultural commodity prices; the state of being equal or equivalent.

parsimonious Excessively frugal; stingy.

partisanship An attitude that always favours one way of feeling or acting especially without considering any other possibilities.

pig iron Crude iron that is the direct product of the blast furnace and that is either refined to produce steel, wrought iron, or ingot iron or is remelted and cast into special shapes.

promulgate To make known openly or publicly; to put into action or force.

reparation Compensation in money or materials payable by a defeated country for damages to or expenditures sustained by another country as a result of hostilities with the defeated country.

social gospel The application of Christian principles to social problems.

speakeasy A place where alcoholic beverages are illegally sold, specifically, such a place during the period of Prohibition in the United States.

statism Concentration of economic controls and planning in the hands of a highly centralized government often extending to government ownership of industry.

suffrage The right of voting.

temperance movement A movement dedicated to promoting moderation and, more often, complete abstinence in the use of intoxicating liquor.

Third International Also known as the Communist International or Comintern, an international communist organization begun in Moscow in 1919 by Vladimir Lenin with the stated purpose of promoting world revolution, but which functioned chiefly as a means by which the Soviet Union exercised control over the international communist movement. The association was dissolved by Joseph Stalin in 1943 during World War II in a move to allay fears of communist subversion among his western allies.

venal Open to corrupt influence and especially bribery.

vicissitude A favourable or unfavourable event or situation that occurs by chance; a fluctuation of state or condition.

World Bank An international organization affiliated with the United Nations, the purpose of which is to finance projects that promote economic development in member nations.

BIBLIOGRAPHY

Useful surveys include David M. Kennedy, *Freedom From Fear: The American People in Depression and War, 1929–1945* (1999); Colin Gordon (ed.), *Major Problems in American History 1920–1945* (1999); Michael E. Parrish, *Anxious Decades: 1920–1941* (1992); and Robert McElvaine, *The Great Depression: America, 1929–1941* (1984). Geoffrey Perrett, *America in the Twenties* (1982), gives extensive overviews of political, social, and cultural aspects of this period. A scholarly history is William E. Leuchtenburg, *The Perils of Prosperity, 1914–32*, 2nd ed. (1993). Daniel Okrent, *Last Call: The Rise and Fall of Prohibition* (2010); and Norman H. Clark, *Deliver Us from Evil* (1976), consider Prohibition. A classic account of politics in the 1930s is William E. Leuchtenburg, *Franklin D. Roosevelt and the New Deal, 1932–1940* (1963). George Lipsitz, *Rainbow at Midnight: Labor and Culture in the 1940s* (1994); and Irving Bernstein, *Turbulent Years: A History of the American Worker, 1933–1941* (1969), are informative accounts of labour during this period. Geoffrey Perrett, *Days of Sadness,*

Years of Triumph (1973, reprinted 1985), comprehensively covers the war years 1939–45. Military history is provided by Kenneth S. Davis, *Experience of War: The United States in World War II* (1965; also published as *The American Experience of War, 1939–1945*, 1967). A comprehensive study is I.C.B. Dear and M.R.D. Foot (eds.), *The Oxford Companion to World War II* (also published as The Oxford Companion to the Second World War, 1995). Civil and military history are discussed in William L. O'Neill, *A Democracy at War: America's Fight at Home and Abroad in World War II* (1993, reissued 1995). Among the useful studies of special topics are Alan Brinkley *Voices of Protest: Huey Long, Father Coughlin, and the Great Depression* (1982); Tetsuden Kashima, *Judgment without Trial: Japanese American Imprisonment during World War II* (2004); Barbara Melosh, *Engendering Culture: Manhood and Womanhood in New Deal Public Art and Theater* (1991); and James N. Gregory, *American Exodus: The Dust Bowl Migration and Okie Culture in California* (1989).

INDEX

Federal Music Project, 32–33
Federal Reserve, 17, 20–21, 24
Federal Theatre Project, 32
Federal Trade Commission, 25
Federal Writers' Project, 32
Fireside Chats, 24–25, 26
Fordney-McCumber Tariff, 4
Fosdick, Harry Emerson, 10
"Four Freedoms," 45
France, 16, 43, 61
Frankfurter, Felix, 54
French Indochina, 47

G

General Motors, 37, 39
Germany, 20, 42, 43, 44, 45, 47, 48, 57, 59,
    60, 61
Glass-Steagall Act, 20–21, 24
gold standard, 20–21
Good Neighbor Policy, 40, 42
Grant, Ulysses S., 4
Grapes of Wrath, The, 18
Great Britain, 20, 43, 44, 45, 46, 59, 61
Great Depression, 12, 15–21, 26, 30, 31, 37, 39, 61

H

Harding, Warren G., 3, 4, 5, 6
Hillman, Sidney, 37
Hiroshima, 59
Hitler, Adolf, 42
Home Owners Loan Act, 25
Hoover, Herbert, 4, 12, 16, 17, 19, 20, 21, 39, 40, 42
Housing Authority, 37
Hughes, Charles Evans, 4
Hull, Cordell, 40

I

Iceland, 44, 45
inflation, 27, 30, 35, 50, 53

International Monetary Fund, 56
Italy, 40, 42, 45, 47, 48, 61
Iwo Jima, 59

J

Jackson, Robert H., 54
Japan, 42, 45, 47–48, 54, 57, 59–60, 61
Japanese Americans, 53–55
Johnson, Hugh S., 24

K

Keynes, John Maynard, 39
Korematsu v. United States, 54
Ku Klux Klan, 7, 10

L

La Follette, Robert M., 6, 66, 68
Landon, Alfred M., 33
League of Nations, 1, 4
Lend-Lease Act, 44, 45
Lenin, Vladimir, 2
Lewis, John L., 37–38
Liberty Bonds, 16
Lincoln, Abraham, 6
Long, Huey P., 30, 31

M

McMahon, Thomas, 37
Mellon, Andrew W., 4, 17
Mississippi Bubble, 16
Missouri, 59
Moley, Raymond, 22
"Monkey Trial," 10
Murphy, Frank, 54
Mussolini, Benito, 42

N

Nagasaki, 59
National Emergency Council, 19